Finding your Sweet Spot

Activate your brain to work on your behalf

By Dr. Harrison S. Mungal

FOREWORD BY DR. DAVID KOCZERGINSKI MD FRCPC
CHIEF OF PSYCHIATRY AND MEDICAL DIRECTOR

WTL INTERNATIONAL

FINDING YOUR SWEET SPOT

Published by
WTL International
930 North Park Drive
P.O. Box 33049
Brampton, Ontario
L6S 6A7 Canada
www.wtlipublishing.com

978-1-927865-27-9

Printed in Canada and in the U.S.A.

Contact author via email: hsmungal@hotmail.com
www.agetoage.ca, www.harrisonandkathleen.com,
www.kissingbreakupsgoodbye.com
Facebook: Harrison Mungal
Twitter: HarrisonandKathleen @HKrelationships, AgetoAge @agetoagec
LinkedIn: Dr. Harrison Mungal PhD
YouTube: Harrison Mungal
Phone: 905-533-1334

who can benefit most from this book?

- Parents, married partners, employers, employees and people in the community at large who feel they haven't yet reached a level of happiness that satisfies them.
- Individuals who feel trapped inside who once thought that by being married they could become free, but instead have found themselves becoming more isolated. They live in fear as they find it difficult to address issues in their relationship and so they live with whatever their spouse decides most of the time.
- Those that feel that they were better off living single as they were happy when they did not have to share "how they feel" with others and were not responsible for making decisions to please others. Although they enjoy being with someone, they prefer their independent life and the freedom they had.
- Individuals that find that before they were married they lived "in a bubble" and find it difficult that their spouse or partner wants them to live outside of it. They feel like their world has changed and they are now being molded by someone else.
- Those who live with social phobias, are passive aggressive or socially awkward. Those who are not sure how to respond to others, become easily anxious or endorse capricious mood, will find this book handy. They will understand why they behave the way they do and what can be done to retrain their brain to become more charismatic and free.
- Those who feel they need more structure or order to their thought lives.
- Mental health or counselling professionals who work with clients that fit the descriptions above.

table of contents

FOREWORD v

INTRODUCTION 1

Your Sweet Spot 5

How the Brain Works 9

The Executive Function 17

Thoughts 23

Quieting the Noisy Brain 27

Organizing your Thoughts 37

Reshaping your Thinking 43

Avoiding Addiction to your Thoughts 53

Focusing on Feelings 63

Feeding the Brain 75

Find What You Love 85

Happiness is a Choice 90

Mind at Ease 95

CONCLUSION: BE GOOD TO YOUR BRAIN 105

ABOUT THE AUTHOR 109

BOOKS WRITTEN BY DR. MUNGAL 110

foreword

Finding your Sweet Spot is a recipe for improving mental health and well-being. This book resonates a message of hope and optimism for individuals who have struggled with emotional distress, relationship conflict, addictions and self-defeating behaviours.

I have known Dr. Mungal for ten years. I have seen him work with many individuals and families in emotional crisis. He has a calm, caring demeanor and a wealth of education and experience which has formed the landscape for the shared knowledge in this book. Trained in theology and social work with two master's degrees and a PhD, he has extensive experience as a clinician, educator and author. Dr. Mungal is a leading expert in the field of cognitive behavioural therapies.

Over decades of work as a psychiatrist in general hospitals, I have had the privilege of offering help to many thousands of individuals presenting to emergency departments in life threatening and life altering states of emotional and behavioral crisis. The most important goals are to engage, instill meaningful hope and provide an early pathway to success. *Finding your Sweet Spot* combines science and psychology in a manner that is both comprehensible and engaging while providing such a path. Overcoming challenge and finding one's "sweet spot" requires motivation and effort. This book provides a thoughtful roadmap to focus efforts for an achievable outcome.

Emotional and behavioral health, not unlike physical health, exist on a continuum. All of us, whether suffering from a debilitating mental illness or simply coping with daily challenges of work, education and relationships, seek strategies to better cope and optimize our well-being and overall functioning. *Finding your Sweet Spot* has helpful insights and strategies for all of us.

This book is grounded in an understanding of neuroscience and evidence based psychotherapies. As an example, mindfulness strategies to quiet a noisy brain or cognitive strategies to focus thoughts and choose happiness are reviewed in a manner that educates, invites and encourages the pursuit of such healthy initiatives.

Dr. Harrison Mungal has shared from his own life experience, education and vast clinical experience in authoring this valuable and insightful book. I believe it will provide inspiration, help and meaning for all readers.

David Koczerginski MD FRCPC
Chief of Psychiatry and Medical Director
Mental Health and Addictions
William Osler Health System

introduction

The idea for this book came to mind after years of noticing patterns while working with individuals, couples and families who struggled in their relationships, parenting, employment and mental health. There were those who appeared to be moving around in circles trying to be the best they could be but not getting anywhere. Then there were others who attempted to move one step forward yet in the process fell back two steps. There were many still who felt like they were stuck in the "mud" of life and could not get out. This group found themselves not moving very much in any direction.

With all the psychoeducation, psychotherapy, support counselling, pastoral counselling, government assistance and community involvement programs, there are many resources invested and many people bending over backwards to support those struggling. However, it appears that the system is a revolving door. Patients come in, are "treated," discharged, and then come in again. Despite all the help, people are still finding it difficult to move ahead in their lives. It is apparent that we are not dealing with the root causes of the issues and are only putting on bandages.

We can see what the effects are and what's behind these effects on a surface level. We can deduce an array of possible solutions. However, we cannot make a person comply with the suggestions being provided. Like the old saying goes, "You can lead a horse to the water but you cannot make it drink." People need suggestions that address the issue and that are promising and sustainable.

I believe when people have a good understanding of how the brain works they will naturally want to be compliant with the advice they are given. People will have a better understanding of how they as individuals function as well as how others do. This

1

FINDING YOUR SWEET SPOT

will enable and encourage them to learn how to accept other people and effectively deal with the behaviours of others. In turn, when a solution is based on a good understanding of how the brain works, it is more effective. It's a recipe for success. Consequently, working from a perspective that acknowledges how the brain functions gives us access to our "sweet spot." The sweet spot is a place in our brains that is tapped into when we find our "groove" in life. It is a place where one inevitably finds happiness.

The core of every issue stems from how we think and what conclusion we allow our minds to draw about life's stimuli. The problems we often encounter are also closely tied to what things occupy our minds that take our focus. We have noticed that after three to six months in a long-term relationship, particularly for those who are married, the brain loses its focus on the relationship. Couples become so busy trying to develop their future together, looking into planning a family, working to shape their career paths, pursuing education and attending to financial commitments that they drift away from their true love. The same applies to parenting. We are very careful about everything that revolves around our first child. When the second or third—or like us, the seventh—comes along, you are far less attentive to the little things. All the ingredients for creating a healthy and happy life come from finding the sweet spot in your brain.

In relationships we see men losing interest in doing the kinds of things it took to get their wives or girlfriends to fall in love with them. Remember the days of buying flowers, being extremely creative in planning dates, looking for restaurants that have a romantic twist, orchestrating special events that created opportunities for you to cuddle and kiss, writing poems, making love notes and the constant communication? Most men admit that they are guilty of not texting, emailing or phoning their spouses nearly as much after they are married. Some men go so far as to say that the longer they are together with their spouse, the less time

2

they spend on such things. To explain this, some men have stated that they are too busy trying to earn an income and taking on the responsibilities of a provider. Others have said they don't see the need to please or pamper their spouse to be as important as when they were first getting to know each other. Some women give the same answers when asked about making an effort to stay close together.

We have found that most women stop pursuing creative ways to keep themselves attractive, especially after they have had their first baby. The woman who used to spend hours looking at herself in the mirror making sure she looked perfect neglects herself when she is married. The signals she used to give off to the one she loved, like the little smirk indicating her interest in intimacy, are less frequent or even stop after being married.

The brain is a magnificent organ which is responsible for our thinking and how we function. This book will focus on the brain and its functions, our thoughts, feelings, behaviours, how to feed our brain and our choices. It will foster a better understanding of why we think the way we do, why we make certain choices we may regret, why we behave the way we do, our weaknesses and our strengths.

This book, when properly applied, will take the relationships of its readers to another level as it teaches individuals to identify their weakest link. When we know what the causes of the disputes in our relationships are, we are able to identify lasting kinds of solutions to create healthier relationships. We cannot ignore our nature and just go about our lives. This leads to trouble. Since problems, disputes, hurts, failures, disconnect and lack of communication all stem from our thinking, understanding how the mind works and the core issues at play will help us to function more effectively, not only in our relationship, but in all areas of life. In achieving this, you will find your sweet spot and the happiness it brings.

FINDING YOUR SWEET SPOT

This book will help you to break free from the fears that have trapped you in a world that is causing issues in your relationship with your partner, your children, other family members, friends, people in your place of employment and elsewhere. You are not alone and it is not impossible to bring light into your world. We have seen many individuals who have tried medications, used many forms of therapies and followed counsellors to no avail finally break free with a brain-centered approach.

If you want to live in peace and happiness and are willing to make a few changes, this book will help you. You will learn how to help yourself and understand others. You will learn how you can bring healing to your body, soul and spirit. You will learn how to live free in your emotions and master your choices by accessing the sweet spot in your brain.

4

YOUR sweet
SPOT

You can scrape by life and experience it as a constant struggle. It is also possible to live your life as a victor. Even when challenges come, you have the right skills to effectively deal with them when you are a victor. Living life this way is what it means to find your sweet spot.

Living in the sweet spot pushes you to take on any challenge regardless of whether you have the skills or not. Your brain becomes programmed to move ahead in life and turns your challenges into opportunities to be successful.

The sweet spot is a wavelength of being that stimulates circuits in the brain that create happy chemicals. It is characterized by feeling confident about who you are, being comfortable or effective in your routines and being more capable of accomplishing the things that make you happy. You have found your sweet spot when you are in the right groove in your life and relationships. You will find that it reduces stress significantly and keeps you in a happy mood. It changes the dynamics of how you live in a noticeable way.

Finding your sweet spot can be very challenging, however once you find it, you will want to surf it all of the time. It's the only spot that gives free access for your brain to function effectively. You see life through a different set of lenses, with purpose and destiny.

FINDING YOUR SWEET SPOT

How people think and communicate is only the tip of the iceberg of the brain's capacity. We all can do more than we perceive: speak more, play more, behave more, influence more, and think more. Most people experience only a taste of what they think or express. Think of achieving your sweet spot as tapping into that greater capacity. A depiction of how society has advanced in its communication technologies over the past twenty years captures the idea of how our brain can advance to operate at greater capacities. About twenty-five years ago, when my wife Kathleen and I were falling in love, we had no cell phones or accessible Internet. Today we have Wi-Fi in most cities and communication can happen anywhere. It is possible that our brains can advance with such profound jumps.

You have found your sweet spot when you are
in the right groove in your life and relationships.

Finding your sweet spot puts your brain at ease as it becomes a lifestyle. It's not just what you can achieve in the extra-personal realm. Finding your sweet spot will greatly impact your relationships. You no longer become overly anxious, react impulsively or operate out of anger towards others. In fact you will refuse to waste energy on being rude to others. You either give facts or walk away from situations that have no benefit to you. You learn to choose your battles in life, fight with the right ammunition, and play your cards right without showing others what's in your hand.

Choosing to live life in the sweet spot changes your perspective on how to live and what you can gain from life. You make choices that are best for you as they bring peace and comfort to your soul. You live life for yourself and your creator along with those close to your heart.

When you learn to "live in the sweet spot," you will find our physical, mental, spiritual, psychological, sexual and social lives to be much happier. You enjoy each component of life that can bring about some measure of pleasure and this keeps you smiling, even when things don't look so great on the outside.

Your sweet spot is neither too hot nor too cold. It is just perfect in every area of your life. You learn how to find honey even when you feel there is none to be found in the situation you face. When your interest, skills and opportunities interact with each other giving a feeling that you were born to be in that spot, you are in the right place. Learning how to achieve the right place in every area of your life is the challenge most people struggle with. They may have all the knowledge, skills and ability, but are unable to pull them all into the right place.

The concept of a "sweet spot" is derived from an understanding that life is short and we need to make the best of it. Every one of us has a place in the brain that can be triggered to make us happy. How can we set off the sweet spot and release happy chemicals? Coming back to another technological illustration, Wi-Fi can be on all the time and can service your phone, tablets, computers and other electronic devices you, your family, friends, colleagues and others enjoy. Our sweet spot can be turned on all of the time in the same way. When it's constantly on, others will see and will want to tap into it and enjoy life with you. How can we create pleasure by our own personal actions? Is this possible? I believe that besides a firm foundation of faith in God, this takes understanding a little about the brains God gave us and how they work.

QUESTIONS TO PONDER

1. How has the advancement of technology expanded our communication? How has this advancement affected our brain?

FINDING YOUR SWEET SPOT

2. How will finding your "sweet spot" in the brain benefit you personally? Will it also affect your relationships?
3. Is it possible to find honey in the most challenging circumstances?
4. When we find our "sweet spot" can others be encouraged or tap in to what we have discovered?

HOW the
brain WORKS

For as long as I can remember, the brain has captured my attention. One day while at work, an aggressive patient became belligerent towards his mother and attacked me, punching me in the head. I had an MRI done and went to the doctor to make sure everything was okay. I had several doctors share their opinions regarding the brain. They shared things we all learn in psychology and psychiatry. One doctor explained that the brain contains billions of nerve cells which coordinate our emotions, sensations, movements, behaviour and thoughts.

From the MRI, the specialist explained that my brain had a one-millimetre indent, however, it was normal for my age. He went on to say that the hit to my head was on the temporal lobe where the brain processes information from my sense of smell, taste and sound, and where it stores memory. He explained that if my head was hit on the frontal lobes it would have affected my short-term memory, movement, planning, organizing, problem solving and thinking. He explained that the parietal lobe affects my sensory nerves such as those that detect taste, touch and temperature and the occipital lobes allow me to process images I see and link them to images stored in my memory.

I was always fascinated about the brain, especially when I went to school and was enrolled in the paramedic program. I was in awe as the teacher shared about it and all the power it held. When I was studying psychology, I was fascinated with all that the brain does in order for a person to function. The fact that it has a network of neurons like electrical wires that are activated when a person is experiencing emotional or physical pain was intriguing. If people were to work together in a network like the brain does, we would definitely have a better world.

You probably remember studying neuroplasticity in high school, which is the ability the brain has to help a person learn new things. The more we repeat something with the attempt to be good at it, the more the brain continues to work to make new neural pathways. In psychology we learn that a person needs to rehearse something about seven times before it is registered in the brain.

Working in psychiatry has taken my fascination to another level. Every day I hear stories of people who function differently as a result of dysfunctional thinking, again, all stemming from the processing of information and how it is applied. Making all attempts to understand why people become paranoid, endorse delusions and hallucinations captured my attention. We know some of the mechanisms behind it, and quite a bit about the physiological actors that play a role, such as the neurotransmitters serotonin and dopamine. The fact that the brain can create beliefs that cannot be verified and that it can effectively operate even when it is compromised, creates a great deal of mystery surrounding the brain and shows that it must be treated with great care.

The more we repeat something with the attempt to be good at it, the more the brain continues to work to make new neural pathways.

I can only assume the passion I have for mental health is a result of the brain and its function. In fact, my first thesis was on the subject of medication and how it affects the brain and the research was said to be phenomenal.

In this chapter, I hope to bring about a basic understanding of the brain and an appreciation of the majesty it has by looking at it from a psychological perspective. I would like to explore the basics of the brain more from an emotional perspective to understand the need to find your sweet spot by considering how you treat your brain. I will share what I have discovered and how it has directed me to find my own sweet spot.

I like to think of the brain as an organization that is run by three main committee members who identify themselves as the hindbrain, the midbrain and the forebrain. The hindbrain is in charge of the brain stem, the spinal cord and a bunch of tissues called the cerebellum. Most of us were taught this in high school. This committee member is in charge of making sure our heart rate and respiration is working as it controls our movement. The midbrain is responsible for our reflex actions, eye movements and voluntary movements.

The forebrain is the biggest part of your brain and is in charge of making sure memory is stored properly. It works with the executive function. It allows you to plan, think, imagine, recognize people and things and play games. The three main committee members are in charge of helping you to function effectively. Once you figure out the purpose of each one of these committee members, it will help you to understand why you are the way you are and how you can work with your mind instead of against it.

The brain has four major lobes, some of which have been briefly detailed. A defect in the temporal lobe, which affects our senses of smell, taste and sound, can hamper our sweet spot. The function of the temporal lobe became evident to me when I worked with Acquired Brain Injury clients. Those whose temporal lobes were affected from a brain injury soon realized that this affected their senses of smell, taste and sound. The food they ate was not as enjoyable, nor was the music they listened to. They lived like robots. When I am feeling like my frontal lobe has been affected, my wife makes comments like, "Wake up and smell the coffee."

When I think of taste, I think of the fact that most of us like tasting things. It allows us to decide what is good for us and what is not. That decision is made by the brain which houses most of the components that give us the ability to do so. Taste is an important aspect of life. We will never really know what is good for us until we try.

What about sounds? Do we give ourselves the time to listen to what is being spoken and consider what sounds we are hearing that trigger our brain? I think sounds are fascinating since they determine how we feel. Sounds can make us happy or sad depending on their frequency. Sounds can affect our moods and change our emotions. You can learn more about sounds and the mind in my book, *Music Therapy and Mental Illness*.

Our brain is like a hub where every nerve registers, similar to a forest where each tree is independent yet connected by its roots. All the nerve cells in our brain are connected along with everything else that makes us function. In a forest you have all the leaves (millions and millions of leaves) that enable the forest to function effectively and all the roots intertwine to have each tree accountable to keeping the forest alive. Our thoughts are the same when the nerves are all registered.

The occipital lobe is another area of the brain, responsible for processing the images we see and connecting them with information we have stored in our memory. If this part of the brain is damaged it can cause blindness. This lobe is important like the others. We as humans typically ask questions when we don't know something, and most things we know are related to what we see.

The next set of lobes are the parietal lobes which, form what I have learned from working with acquired brain injury clients, are responsible for touch, movements, taste and temperature. I remember these lobes particularly well because most of the clients I worked with were affected in their parietal lobes. I had clients who would walk outside with just a t-shirt on (or sometimes with no shirt) during the winter when it was -27°C, because the sun was bright and they assumed that it was summer. They had no sense of temperature. I also had clients who could not taste their food. Sometimes they would get frustrated with what they saw on their plate not knowing how it tasted. With their memory affected, there were times the food was taken away, rearranged on the plate, and the client thought it was new food and they would then eat.

Then there is the frontal lobe. Remember, the frontal lobe affects short-term memory. I have heard some physicians say that short-term memory can store about seven—twenty to thirty-second memories at a time. The storage is very fragile and with distraction, the information being retrieved can easily be lost. Some of us prefer not to remember traumatizing incidents. It is interesting how the brain sometimes has ways of burying such memories as a defense mechanism.

A hit on the frontal lobe can affect our movement in addition to short-term memory. Planning, organizing and problem solving are other areas of the brain that could be affected by a hit to the frontal lobe.

This is one lobe I talk about a lot because it's the lobe out of which the "executive function" operates. This lobe is responsible for scheduling, reasoning and planning; it's a short-term storage site. The lobe is also responsible for controlling voluntary movements. Interestingly, when clients are disorganized, passive and present with short memory, the executive function hasn't much to work with. Usually, I would recommend developing routines, planning and organizing, while challenging clients to give reasons for actions and as a result I would see self-development. I see these clients beginning to focus more and once they find their sweet spot, it's like they've jumped off a springboard.

FINDING YOUR SWEET SPOT

In psychology, we learn that Sigmund Freud believed that our behaviour is impacted significantly by events in our childhood. I can attest to this as I see how many young people's lives are affected by events that took place when they were children. Our childhood experiences and subconscious mind determine our behaviour and how we think. Children who were traumatized by events or abused (emotionally, sexually, physically and verbally) all have related consequences they face in functioning as an adult.

I like to think of the brain as being a music band or a grand orchestra with lots of musical instruments all organized into sections. Each section has its own tune to play and once every instrument is working in harmony the orchestra can function as it should. An orchestra needs a conductor who can lead each section to perform its job. This conductor, I like to call the conscience. Sometimes there may be certain instruments in an orchestra that are out of tune as a result of not being cleaned properly or because they have not been put to practice enough and these instruments become rusty.

When I speak with patients, I usually give an analogy that the brain is like a wall made with bricks. Each brick is placed from the time of birth. Unfortunately those bricks can become weakened by life's stressors such as pressure from school, finances, relationships, parenting, career choices, bullying, assaults, abuse, trauma, addictions and medicine. When a brick is loosened by these stressors, we need to secure it in place to make sure the brick stays in the right position.

We use medications, counselling, spirituality, exercise, vacation, family support and other coping strategies as mortar to keep our bricks in place. I found that love is one of the most effective mortars along with professional support. The goal is to use all the necessary support to keep the bricks in place so the brain can function effectively. If the brick falls out, it weakens the entire brain and could cause permanent damage.

14

Unfortunately I have seen many individuals who purposely refuse to take care of their brains and they live life in an unhealthy state. I have seen families refuse to give the support needed for their loved ones, or refuse the recommended support as they themselves don't understand the long-term effects of a loose brick.

If you look at the brain as two hemispheres, left and right, you can see that each half has a different job or function. If one half is affected, the other half is affected. Both hemispheres need to be functioning healthily in order for the individual to make rational decisions, live purposefully and in harmony with the world around them.

I like comparing the hemisphere to couples. In order to survive and live in a happy healthy relationship, both parties in the relationship need to function in sync with one another. The brain is like a family who works together. If each person fulfills their role, the family will remain healthy.

Did you know that it is not just defects and injuries that can affect our brain? There are other things we do that can affect how effectively our brain works and can impact how close we get to that sweet spot.

The brain is like a fancy computerized or digital device. It can do many things and is resilient. But like the laptop, your brain has vulnerabilities. You have to treat it in the right way to get the best out of it. You wouldn't pour water over your laptop. It's not designed for that! Similarly, there are things you should and shouldn't do to help your brain function at a higher level and emit those happy chemicals.

Our next chapter takes a closer look at the executive function so that we can further understand the idea of the brain as a complex organ that needs to be treated the right way through our choices, words, actions and involvements as well as the way we structure our lives.

FINDING YOUR SWEET SPOT

QUESTIONS TO PONDER

1. The brain has the ability to help a person learn new things. How many times does a person need to speak or rehearse something in order for the brain to register it?
2. If the brain is considered an organization who would be the three main committee members?
3. What happens when the temporal lobe is affected?
4. From what lobe does the executive function operate? How can developing routines help those affected in this part of the brain?
5. Explain the analogy of the brain being like a brick wall.

the executive
FUNCTION

The executive function, housed in the frontal lobe, is one of the most fascinating parts of the brain. I grew an interest in it even from a young age while in high school studying biology.

The executive function is a very important part of the brain that many people have not yet tapped into fully and have been utilizing it on a limited scale. I believe when this part of the brain is being used effectively, we see less issues in relationships with family members, in our friendships, in our place of employment and in the community in general.

When I think of the word "executive," my thoughts reflect on someone dressed in formal wear who looks important and carries out a high level of responsibility. I picture someone who has high authority and power, sets rules and gives orders: someone who is instrumental in driving a company to succeed, who pursues to achieve a mission, vision and objective.

The executive function of the brain takes on a similar role. It is detail-oriented. When this function is not working properly, it affects one's ability to function independently, pursue a career path or move ahead.

FINDING YOUR SWEET SPOT

I ran two charities and a not-for-profit organization, and as the lead person, it was my responsibility to gather information, formulate policies and procedures, set structure and order, and keep the organization and its workers focused and on track. I see this to be similar to the executive function of the brain—to keep you focused and on track. There were many times when it was tempting to be driven by others, adapt other visions and be distracted. These distractions are like the many thoughts that present themselves that can set our brains off course. I found the organizations to be more fruitful when I stayed focused.

The executive function will help you to make wise decisions from your past experience and remind you of the consequences of your choices. The choice is ultimately yours. When touching a hot stove for the first time, you feel the pain but it helps you decide if you should touch it again. The executive function will remind you of the experience and the choice should be to avoid it.

The executive function is divided into two main groups. There is the regulation group which deals with changing behaviour as a result of our surroundings and how we respond to them. And the other is the organizational group which processes information that is gathered and evaluates it. It helps to structure information so we can function effectively.

The executive function will help you to make
wise decisions from your past experience and
remind you of the consequences of your choices.

When the executive function is working well, an individual will be able to give answers within seconds. They will not show struggles in processing information or developing a plan.

Individuals who find it challenging to start a task or have difficulty in working within a time frame show signs of impaired

18

executive function. Those who tend to try to get things done quickly or who do things very slowly and often incompletely, in my experience, most likely have a problem with their executive function.

Working in mental health has enabled me to put into practice the studies I did with the executive function when I was in university. There are many people who can be impaired in the prefrontal cortex of the brain from accidents or from birth. Individuals with learning disabilities, depression, ADHD, stroke, ABI and Alzheimer's-related illness show problems with the executive function.

When the executive function is affected because of genetics, its effects can be detected from the time a child starts school. I personally don't believe this is permanent since the brain is still in development. The ability to do a good job comes with life experience and skill development. Anyone with an issue with their executive function can outgrow it with training. But we see that people with an impairment of the executive function either by trauma or other genetic causes often struggle with certain consequences.

The mental skills the executive function coordinates assist the brain to organize and act on information received. Some people have difficulty multitasking or are unable to complete projects. They have a willingness to be productive with lots of ideas and good intentions, but have difficulty managing their time.

As a counsellor, one way I found to understand an individual's difficulties is to assess how the processes of executive function are working. I analyze the causes of the issues presented, the effects they have on the individual and those around them, and how the patient processes solutions. Assessing how the individuals conduct their daily lives, how they analyze problems, how they handle issues, and how they attempt to arrive at solutions brings about a better understanding of their executive function.

FINDING YOUR SWEET SPOT

Issues with the executive function should not be considered a disability, but rather a weakness in mental skills. The brain is very plastic (capable of improving) so there is always hope.

When assessing an individual for whether their executive function is impaired, I look to see if when interrupted, they lose their train of thought. I look for evidence that they have difficulty embracing change, making decisions and expressing ideas in detail. An inability to do multiple tasks at one time and difficulty processing how others feel are also signs I look for.

Then there are those who can be very impulsive. They find it challenging to stop, think and react. They make impulsive decisions and most of the time, regret what they have said or done. Some examples are: spending money without processing whether there is a need or becoming argumentative without considering facts. The commercial stores have learned strategies to attract customers, especially those who have underdeveloped executive functions.

I have seen clients who have trouble learning rules and making simple decisions. Many are unmotivated, endorse inappropriate social behaviours, are unable to monitor their own performance in life, and have little to no insight into their self-awareness. If a superior in an organization were to find these issues in an executive, he or she would quickly be replaced.

Rehabilitating the executive function can be challenging especially when the individual makes little or no acknowledgment of the need for support. However, when the individual is on board, training or retraining the brain to develop the areas of weakness will enhance the executive function to do its job and this has been successful in many instances.

The men I worked with who were suffering with ABI used to be asked to plan their schedule on a daily basis and discuss it in detail. We created a checklist of all the things that needed to be completed for the day, the week and the month, and developed

20

routines from the moment they woke up in the morning to the time they went to bed.

One point I want to stress is that you don't have to have a disease to have the need to improve your executive function. Just like an orchestral music instrument can get rusty, our executive function can get rusty from underuse, distractions or the wrong kinds of stimulation. Learn to use whatever tools you may have available to you to develop and manage your executive function even if that is professional assistance.

Next, we will consider our thoughts. We all have them and some struggle with keeping them lined up like ducklings. Thoughts often have the tendency to stray and wander. Our thoughts can look more like a salad than ducklings in a row. They can be scattered and uniform. They can be clear and focused too. We will learn some ways to work with our brain to achieve this in the chapters that follow.

QUESTIONS TO PONDER
1. What do you think of when you hear the word "executive function"?
2. What is the main job of the executive function?
3. Can a person with an issue with their executive function overcome it?
4. Think of some ways to improve your executive function.

THOUGHTS

This short chapter sets the stage for the next few chapters which focus on your thoughts. What are thoughts? We all have them and they travel with us as long as we are awake. We cannot run away from them as they live inside of us. Thoughts are fed by what we see, hear, smell, taste and touch. They are affected by our emotions. Some say they live in the conscious mind and maintain their livelihood by opinions, beliefs and ideas gathered from the five senses that are part of the host's well-being.

Thoughts are what allow a person to make sense of the world they live in and what they experience. Thoughts can be changed with new information that is gathered. They create attitudes and shape our beliefs that have been formed from the environment, our experiences, skill-building and education acquired.

Thoughts can be disproportionately skewed towards perception, which means it is possible to have too many perception-based thoughts. These are thoughts that correlate directly with what we see, hear, smell, taste and touch. This can control the life of the person who carries them or even someone else's depending on the personality and character of the person. There should be a balance between thoughts stimulated by perception and other types of thoughts.

FINDING YOUR SWEET SPOT

When a thought comes to mind, the mind has the choice to store it in its memory or not. The decision to store a thought usually depends on how important it is to the person.

Thoughts are what allow a person to make sense of the world they live in and what they experience.

Thoughts are closely tied to emotions. If a present thought is associated with a thought from the past, it will stir up an emotion that was registered with the past thought. The current thought will become stimulated to bring the past thought alive. The memory associated with that emotion will create a world of thoughts that were associated with that past thought. Our thoughts are connected to emotions and trigger other thoughts like the web of a spider.

Thoughts are fueled and developed from the amount of attention we give them. A thought can become multiple thoughts if we give it too much attention. The dominant thought likes to be the centre of attention and it will want to be used to justify every other idea that comes to the mind.

It's not difficult to imagine how one thought can trigger many thoughts. I could have a thought to buy flowers for my wife on Valentine's Day. It doesn't just stop there. I think about how spending $55.00 on twelve steams of roses compares with the $19.95 I usually spend on regular days. Several other thoughts come into my mind such as *Everyone else is spending that kind of money. Buy the flowers. Red flowers and a box of chocolates will lead to good sex. Buy the flowers. Your wife deserves more than $55.00's worth of roses since she birthed your seven children. Buy the flowers. You have a tradition of giving flowers to your wife and daughters. Buy the flowers.* Or, *Flowers are for young lovers. Don't buy the flowers. Take her out to dinner instead. Don't buy the flowers. It's cheaper to give flowers a week before Valentine's*

Day. Don't buy the flowers on Valentine's Day. You buy flowers almost every month. Don't buy the flowers, etc.

Individuals struggling with addictions, anxiety and depression carry more thoughts in their minds than others. Those with addiction issues think of all the reasons they could justify their use with a main thought that justifies the thought, *"It will be the last time."* Those with anxiety may struggle with a central thought about a traumatic incident in the past, triggering similar thoughts from the memory and newly formed associated thoughts. Those with depression may have a thought of "no hope" which fuels all manner of thoughts of sadness and self-harm which the idea of no hope justifies.

Taking control of dominant thoughts is the first step to strengthening the mind and re-training your thinking patterns. It can bring healing to your emotional life. We need to look at becoming champions over our thoughts in order to conquer our addictions, anxieties and depression. Champions are not born champions; they are made champions and conquering your thoughts will not necessarily come naturally. It will require practice and an investment of time.

When a thought comes into the mind that produces no semblance of fruitfulness or that should not hold a position of importance, a seasoned champion will not allow it to create other thoughts. Thoughts like: *I feel like a failure; Nobody understands me; What's the purpose anyway?* are not entertained. Every situation is analyzed and pondered upon if needed. The end result is that there is now an environment in the mind where the sweet spot can be accessed.

In this next chapter, I will talk about quieting the brain when our thought-life becomes too active. This is important as it will help the one who has conquered their thoughts get one step closer towards the goal of finding his or her sweet spot.

QUESTIONS TO PONDER

1. How are thoughts fed?
2. Can we change our thoughts?
3. Are thoughts closely tied to emotions? Explain how.
4. How can we be champions of our thoughts?

quieting **the**
NOISY brain

Working in mental health, I hear many patients share about their noisy brain. Some express that they can hear their own thoughts. Some say they can hear their conscience or God, and others say they can hear other people's voices. We all have thoughts we hear if we focus on them.

Most people can say they hear their thoughts if they pay close attention to themselves. People who think a lot can hear themselves planning what should be done next, what they should do to solve a problem, what meeting they need to attend, who they need to meet, etc.

With the amount of complaints that go around during casual talk in today's culture, a typical conversation can easily sway towards a negative tone unless someone brings it back to a positive one. People's sinful nature speaks of everything that is negative. The glass is always half empty in the eyes of most.

We hear couples complain from the moment they walk through the door for counselling. They talk about the traffic, the children, the people they saw on their way to the clinic, their family members who called during the week, their boss, their colleagues, their pastor, their spouse, their children, their finances, their housing, their career, their education, their vacation, their shopping experiences, and so on. And in all this talking, there are more negative identifying factors than positive.

FINDING YOUR SWEET SPOT

The brain soaks in all of this. These are triggers that set the brain on a course of becoming noisy. The result is an unhappy individual.

From working with individuals who are suffering with schizophrenia, I am always flabbergasted when I hear their stories of the voices in their heads or the thoughts they hear and the conversations they carry on with. After doing eighteen months of research on schizophrenia, I have learned to appreciate this illness and those who are struggling with it.

Even without illness, people have struggles with their thoughts on a daily basis. I once heard a mental health speaker say that our brains carry over forty thousand thoughts per day.

Schizophrenia is an illness that interferes with a person's ability to think clearly as they can be out of touch with reality. Schizophrenia affects a person's thoughts which affect their emotions. This impairment can create delusions, paranoia and hallucinations. A person can develop a fixed belief of an auditory hallucination where they hear multiple voices affecting their mental status. The brain becomes noisy to the point that the individual can become agitated and aggressive, having to control the voices and what they are telling them to do.

I consider the normal brain to be quite noisy since it's always thinking and never stops. Inner conversations are constantly transpiring in the mind. We think about what we see, hear, smell and taste. We think of the present, the past and the future. There comes a point where it is too much.

A noisy mind is characterized by involuntary thinking. Most people have learned to live with the noise as it's their norm. This habit we develop is deeply embedded in our mind and it becomes our way of life. It's like being born with nine fingers or eleven toes, we get used to it and we see it as natural.

We all go through the effects of the noisy brain when we have a lot of issues to deal with as well as day to day things to do.

When you are told your boss wants to see you, all the possible reasons play in your mind. Some people are unable to sleep the day before meeting with their boss as they think about what they might have done wrong. Some people, on the other hand, think of all the credits they should receive from their boss only to find out they were being disciplined.

Think of having to be in court and all the thoughts that your brain conjures up that pull you down. Your anxiety level rises as you stand in the unknown world not knowing what will happen. I have had clients who freaked out and didn't show up as they were unable to face a judge or be in that form of atmosphere after all their negative thoughts had circulated.

What about simply writing an exam paper and thinking of all the things you did wrong after? Your mind thinks of all the better ways you could have studied and how you should have done your answers differently.

What about some of you who may be addicted to things you are ashamed to disclose with your family, spouse, friend or others who may care about you? You do it secretly with the hope that no one will find out. Then you justify it in your mind with all the reasons why you do it. As the addiction takes a hold of your life, your brain thinks of all the things you would say if you were ever found out. The battle of the brain continues until you have your way and no one finds out about your weakness. As it continues, your brain thinks of all the things you would say and this goes on until you quit or are found out.

What about driving down the highway? You know you should not speed. However, your brain goes through all the things you will say to the police officer if you are caught speeding. You try to justify your reason for speeding with excuses you heard worked for others. Your brain constantly thinks of all the things you would say.

FINDING YOUR SWEET SPOT

What about attending an important meeting? Throughout the meeting you think of all the things you want to say, all the questions you want to ask. However, for the life of you, you feel insecure and when it's your turn to speak, you do not say what you had been spending all of that time thinking? Then the meeting comes to a close and you become frustrated with yourself as you reflect on it and think of all the things you should have said.

You may have been shopping and someone said something that was upsetting. You think of all the things you should have said though you leave without saying a word. You feel like you're a loser and your mind plays words that make you feel angry and upset. You reach your car in the parking lot and do one of two things: you either scream and yell like a crazy person or cry as you think how much the words bothered you.

Another example is being out with your family when some strange person yells at your spouse or your child or they make racial comments. Maybe they even took the last cookie which your child was heading towards. You call your spouse or child but do not address the person. Your mind thinks of all the things you should have done or said and the thoughts make you feel defeated. Alternatively, you may have spoken up and wish you did not say something you said. Again your mind goes over and over what you should have done.

Picture your child staying out late at night. Parents often think about all the negative things that could go wrong, especially if they themselves did something that was not acceptable or pleasing to their parents. You can't sleep and are restless as your brain thinks of all the things your child may be doing. As your child comes home you might get up and start yelling and screaming, sometimes making wrongful accusations.

We all have examples of what the brain thinks which at times can be quite noisy. The more free-time we have on our hands, the more we give the brain the option of thinking and with excess thinking, comes the noise. We can start a conversation with the brain from anything we focus on. It's not always about problems or issues we face in life.

Some people have expressed that they think of so many things it makes it difficult to settle their mind. Some need to use medications to keep the brain from working too much. When the brain becomes noisy and the thoughts cannot stop, the individual is unable to sleep. Some people are awake for most of the night as their thoughts continue to work on their behalf, thinking and never stopping. They have set a habit of over-thinking in their brains. It affects their eating habits and their ability to concentrate, and it keeps them restless.

The more free-time we have on our hands,
the more we give the brain the option of thinking
and with excess thinking, comes the noise.

The only time we are not thinking about the noise in our heads is when we go to sleep, however the moment we wake up, the noise begins as we plan our day or think about how the day will pan out. You begin coordinating your appointments, activities that involve your children or your spouse, your "to do list," chores and everything else that you will be faced with that day. Our mind fusses about every detail like when we are on a first date, except in this case, the thoughts and worries are not reserved for such occasions. They're constant.

The noisy brain sometimes has difficulty settling down and as a result, over time, it makes it difficult to go to sleep. Some people are awake for most of the night as their thoughts continue to work on their behalf, thinking and never stopping. They have set a habit of over-thinking in motion.

Sometimes it may appear that the thought or the inner voice in our mind is like a broken record that keeps playing over and over again. It constantly analyzes all that you do, say and want to say. Everyone you meet and all the circumstances you encounter play and replay.

Negative thoughts tend to take up a disproportionate amount of space in the mind. They may be along the lines of worry, stress or unresolved issues which create frustration and anger.

Most people can acknowledge extra noise in their brains when they are asked if they ever have thoughts of solutions to a problem while engaged in a conversation with someone. Sometimes someone is speaking to us and we tune them out and focus on unrelated thoughts.

Some may experience unwanted thoughts being triggered by a traumatic event in the past and find that a current environment or words associated with that trauma may bring a flashback. When that happens, the mind formulates thoughts which we may not say verbally but we reflect.

Then there are some who always analyze other people's situations, behaviour and reactions. They allow their minds to work constantly as they assess people with their minds. How others dress, walk, look and smell become an obsession.

Some people like to daydream. They spend most of their time allowing their minds to be over-stimulated by music, emails, surfing the net, gaming and so on and carry on fantasy storylines in their heads.

Thinking too much can prevent us from having opportunities to build friendships with others including our family members. We can lose touch with what is happening around us. How many of us have experienced driving down the road, and we could not recall how we got from point A to point B as our minds were busy with thoughts? Some people have missed highway exits as they were busy thinking about cars on the road or what happened that day. Imagine living with someone and you have this habit of drifting off into endless thoughts. You'd miss out on countless opportunities to form connections with that person.

Most people could be more productive if they switched on and off their minds at appropriate times, but the mind cannot be controlled by a switch. However, we *can* control the mind to quiet it down which brings inner peace and stimulates that sweet spot.

We all need to learn how to relax the brain and focus on one thing at a time. The mind will roam and go as far as you allow it to travel. Here are some great ways to reign in your thoughts and to reduce the mind from over-thinking:

- Meditate. Learn to take five to ten minutes a day where you can be alone, sit down, take a few deep breaths and keep focused on breathing. Clear your mind of any thoughts and try to keep it calm. You can then take one word that is positive and focus only on that word and see how you can implement it in your day. I usually give one word every day to our children to apply to their day. Only one word.

- Focus on one activity at a time. As much as I like to multi-task, it can be very challenging and taxing on the brain. Do one thing at a time and put all your effort into it. This way, you're not overworking your brain and you don't have to question whether you gave the task your all.

- Think positively and let go of the negative things you are thinking. Our nature feeds negative thinking. We need to learn how to let go and take the moment as it comes. We can never be prepared enough, so take what you have and deal with the issue as it comes. Preparing unnecessarily can cause your mind to work overtime.

- Be open-minded. So many people think they know it all and don't give themselves time to listen. Learn to be open-minded and learn from others even if they are wrong. Look at what you can learn from someone rather than what you need to tell them. You can slow your mind down by listening to others.

- Learn to laugh. When I laugh, I don't think of how funny I am. Others may think that for me. When we laugh it's good medicine for the soul. It clears the mind and stirs up the good emotions we carry. It will make your day a pleasant one.

- Set reasonable goals and work towards accomplishing them. When we are working towards something, we feel good, especially when we finish. Once the mind is aware that you are working towards something, it will drive your thoughts to be progressive. We all want to feel like champions. Aim at goals that you can conquer.

- Learn to observe what you are thinking and steer the thought to something useful. No one can read your mind, so no need to feel discouraged or sad. Retrain your mind to focus on something positive when you observe your thoughts are not what they should be.

The brain can be quite noisy but yet controlled. We need to learn how to think and allow thoughts to fade and move on to another topic. We should never be so caught up with thoughts that we carry a conversation with ourselves. If you don't stop yourself, such a conversation can last for hours.

Quieting your thoughts is of utmost importance. We cannot afford to let our brain get overloaded. This will impair our ability to be able to focus and figure our way through life's tensions and stressors.

I used to watch my wife read a book and think, *How can she be so still and just read?* In reality, when she reads her brain is settled yet noisy as it tries to visualize what is being read and paint a picture or create a movie in her mind. Reading is actually quite relaxing and can be beneficial in training the brain to maintain a capacity of noise that is healthy because it is organized around one theme and it is focused. This leads to the next chapter which talks about organizing your thoughts. Like a filing cabinet, our brain thrives in an organized environment. Our thoughts need to be organized.

QUESTIONS TO PONDER

1. What are some triggers cause the brain to be noisy?
2. What are some characteristics of a noisy brain?
3. Can you relate to any of the examples given? Describe some similar situations you have experienced?
4. What are some great ways to reign in your thoughts and to prevent the mind from over-thinking?

organizing
your THOUGHTS

The brain is like a computer that needs structure in order for it to function effectively. It looks for ways to stay organized in order to keep settled and focused. When thoughts are organized, you can sleep in peace with an assurance that everything will be okay. As you saw in the "How the Brain Works" and "The Executive Function" chapters, the brain's design and function is very organized. Each area of the brain has specialized roles and information is stored according to a certain layout. You can help your brain in arriving at your sweet spot by conducting your thoughts and lives in an organized way. Let's explore.

Kathleen and I meet with several couples that express that they are unable to sleep as their lives are so disorganized. Their families are dysfunctional and they desperately need some form of structure. They cannot stop thinking about the stressors that are building up, affecting their relationship and the people around them. They find it difficult to organize their thoughts, especially when employment, family and finances are part of the problem. They are unable to share their feelings with their spouse, as they are afraid of their reactions. They become stressed out. Even though to some looking from the outside it appears to be a simple issue, to those struggling it's like a hurricane.

Some individuals appear to be frazzled in their thoughts like they are in a maze contest looking for a way out. They become busy trying to figure out their life, while others around them drift into new relationships. When they are ready to deal with reality, it becomes too late and issues pop up in their relationships like pimples on someone's cheek.

When I started to work three jobs some time ago, the process of time management and organizing my thoughts became a necessity. I would double book myself with work and events with friends. I had little to no time with Kathleen and the children, little to no time for myself or others, and saw my parents and extended family once or twice a year.

I had to learn how to organize my thoughts when my lifestyle was affecting my relationship. I started to think very negatively about life to the point where I did not see a purpose for living. I felt that my relationship was more for Kathleen and the children, working to make ends meet and having no time to enjoy life.

The negative thoughts crippled me and I lived in a bubble for many years. It was safer for me to hide myself in work than to be at home and live in the reality of raising a family. Working and bringing in an income was easier than to have idle hands and get myself into trouble.

Life is not about just working and fun, it's about using time wisely. When we can set priorities, we can organize our thoughts knowing that things will be completed. Our thoughts race when we have had a history of forgetting important details in life. Have you ever forgotten to pay your credit card bill on time? Forgot an important event? Forgotten date night with your spouse?

Sometimes our thoughts can be like letters that are waiting to be put together into words. Like the game Scrabble, where you put the letters together to make a word, sometimes our thoughts and lives need arranging and organizing. The problem people have is not finding the right letters in the brain to create words, or not finding the right words to create sentences. Sometimes it's because we are either too lazy or become codependent where our spouse thinks for us. Other times, we just get overwhelmed by all of the plans we have for ourselves—all of the letters we are working with that we must use up.

Learning to live with your thoughts can be frightening at times, since your thinking can lead to issues that will eventually affect your relationship and your future. We recommend for individuals who are living with negative thoughts to learn how to be creative in organizing them to live a stress-free life. Later in this book I will talk about cognitive behavior therapy (CBT) and dialectical behavior therapies (DBT). It will give a better understanding about positive and negative thoughts.

Organizing your thoughts is really about organizing your life. Organizing your thoughts to reduce stress, starts with organizing your time. First organize your day, then your week, then your month, then a few more months. Set out your goals for the year and then for a few years after that. Be specific about how you will accomplish your goals and fill in details of your plan accordingly.

Kathleen and I encourage couples to start by finding a time that works best for them for logging their thoughts. Some people find it's better at night, so they can sleep in peace knowing that they will not forget important details. Some choose the morning, when their thoughts are fresh. Choosing a time is very important as your brain will be looking forward to meeting with you. It's like when you have a routine of eating or sleeping. Your brain reminds you when, and once adhered to, you feel content.

The next step in the process is to empty your brain of everything you are thinking—all your ideas, concerns, questions, feelings, plans—and focus on one subject. Choose how you will log your information so that you can recall it when you need it but in a way that will give the brain rest. We need to learn how to relieve the brain from working too much, so consider this as you choose how to record your ideas, thoughts, questions, concerns and chores. When I was younger, I would use a tape recorder or a voice recorder and share my thoughts to myself so I could remember what I needed to do. Now we can use Microsoft Outlook and other programs as reminders. This will help you to stop worrying and reduce anxiety.

In this present day, I send a text to myself, call Kathleen and remind her of what I need to do, keep a notepad in my car and by my bed, or use my phone's voice recorder. I send emails to myself and try to keep all my ideas and things to do in one place. Kathleen has a book which we both use for the family.

If you were to buy a house or go on a vacation, it would be very important to organize your thoughts otherwise you would be flustered and overwhelmed. In buying a house, you would consider your income and expenses, your down-payment, bank loan, personal loan, the area you want to live, and the type of home you are looking for. You would not just find a house and decide you want to buy it without consideration of these things. If you did, you would soon find yourself panicking, especially if you know others are interested in the house and you have no idea of what is needed to buy the house.

To get the best out of a vacation, you would need to plan and organize your thoughts about what you want to do, what you can do and what you cannot do. You would look into every option to make it a memorable vacation. If you jump in your car and drive to your destination, there are many things that can become challenging and your thought process can be disturbed.

If you ever had to give a speech, teach or even go in front of a crowd to say hello, you have to process your thoughts regarding what you will be saying. You write short notes as a reminder of what to say and these notes connect your thought process. Our brain has a sense of release when we are able to articulate our thoughts. The sweet spot in the brain will produce confidence and self-esteem. You will notice you are braver and bolder and the sense of anxiety fades away.

Go ahead and write down your thoughts, ideas and plans down to the very hour. Revise them and you will see that they get more organized each time. Your actions will follow suit once you have a plan in place and then so will your thoughts. Happy chemicals will be released from your newly found order and the sense of achievement you get from accomplishing things you have set out to on a daily basis.

Your brain is an organized organ that works in a highly organized way. Don't confuse your brain by having a disorganized life, which leads to disorganized thoughts. Planning your life ahead of time and in a detailed manner and setting routines helps the executive function of your brain. If you want to hit that sweet spot, introduce some more order into your life by putting this into practice.

Your brain is an organized organ that works in a highly organized way. Don't confuse your brain by having a disorganized life, which leads to disorganized thoughts.

In this next chapter, I want to focus on our thinking patterns. Some of us have shaped our minds to think negatively more so than positively. We cannot see the good in anything and our world appears to be all negative. Everything we say or do, or what others have to say or have done, is all negative. It becomes how we come across to others since our thoughts are not filtered. On the other hand, we can be optimistic and have a positive view. This can only come by taking control of our thinking process.

FINDING YOUR SWEET SPOT

QUESTIONS TO PONDER

1. How can learning to organizing our thoughts help us in our relationships. What happens when we allow negative thoughts to take a front seat in relationships?
2. What is the first step in organizing your thoughts?
3. How can we use technology to empty our brain of everything we are thinking?
4. Think of some ways that will help you organize your thoughts and your relationships.

reshaping
your THINKING

This chapter covers a subject that was also touched on in the "Quieting the Noisy Brain" chapter. It can be said that we all have two forms of thinking, positive and negative. Some people are very negative and may not readily realize it as they have lived with it for so long. A negative perspective appears to be something positive for them and they may not see how it affects their livelihood. Many such people cannot see the positive side of anything and this leads to an unhealthy, bitter life.

Negative thinking has lasting effects on the mind which affect our health. You may have heard that "stress is a killer" and it is. In the extreme case, negative thinking leads people to kill themselves as they lose hope, especially hope for their future. But even on a more subtle level, negative thinking is suspected to have an association with negative physical outcomes brought on by stress.

We all have to determine what our outlook will be—whether we are optimistic or pessimistic. There is no other alternative and no one else can make the choice for us. The outlook one has on life is determined by our thinking and our attitudes. Someone who is pessimistic can learn how to live positively by changing their thinking and attitudes.

Thinking the best of people and every situation you approach can be challenging until it becomes a lifestyle. Positive thinking is like watching your weight or striving for healthy eating. It can be a struggle until you see the purpose.

Some clients have mentioned that they cannot see any good in their spouse or in their child and feel what's best for them is to walk away rather than to fight. They often blame others and it's common to hear them share about their life being affected by the other people in their circle. The negative conversations or "gossip" that they are immersed in has made them the way they are. Some people have become so negative that their thoughts are heavily concentrated in that they have no room for light to enter in. Everything that comes out of their mouth is negative. Even though you may not find anything wrong, they will. They will pick on every issue, from the way others dress to how others walk and talk. It never stops. They themselves have low self-esteem and cannot see beyond their own life. They assume everyone is like them while they don't have much to live for or talk about.

In order to find the sweet spot, you must be a positive thinker. You have to train your brain or else you're going to have a very hard time finding your sweet spot.

Like I explain to our clients and even our own children, "All things work together for good." That means you have to learn how to look at finding the positives, even if things are not looking the way you expected. It can be difficult to find the good when your child is involved in a motor vehicle accident. It can be a big challenge to find the good when a family member or your close friend is unable to bear children. How do you see the good when you are unemployed and have no money to buy food? Although it is challenging, it is possible to find the good in every situation.

We know it is God's perfect will for us to have all that He has created for us and learn how to trust Him. If your son got into a motor vehicle accident, you can look at the fact that he will learn to never to speed on the road. You can appreciate that he should not have been texting while driving. He might learn that there are dangerous drivers on the road and that he really needs to be more careful when driving to avoid a worse outcome.

If your family member or close friend is unable to bear children, nothing stops you from praying, however, consider that maybe God sees the future of the children that would result. Maybe they might be a better surrogate, adoptive or foster parent. Throwing in the towel does not solve the issues and being negative about it does not help either. Who knows? It could save some children who might otherwise end up living on the streets.

When I was unemployed, it was very humbling. We lived on used clothes, ate out very rarely and purchased food that was marked down and definitely not made by the favoured brand names. It taught us a lesson to appreciate those who don't have and better equipped us to teach them how to survive with little.

We still never complained and to others it looked as though we were working for good money. We kept the children clean and healthy. They ate the right food and we survived. Never complaining, but taking advantage of our disadvantage, we spent more time together and we got to know each other quite well.

We became more involved in volunteering in the community and church to occupy our time. I did many community courses to train myself, learned how to ice skate and swim. I took whatever job came my way. I worked as a drywall taper, as a worker in group homes with men who were developmentally delayed, and as a photo technician for Woolco. I sold insurance packages and vacuums, volunteered at a provincial prison, worked nightshifts with men who were on federal parole and worked with young offenders.

We looked at the positive in all of these circumstances, even when we could not afford the best gifts for our children. We are proud of them making the right choices in life today. We have two in school for social work, one in school for psychiatry and one who is a nurse. The others are still in the process of finding out their career paths.

None of our children have been into drugs or alcohol, were rebellious, or chose to live on the street. They haven't sold their bodies for money or drugs and not one of them was difficult to manage. They learn to appreciate life and the positive attitude Kathleen and I bring to them takes them far. We encourage them to be the best in all they do and we stress that their choices will determine their outcomes even if things might look like they're going wrong for a time.

Positive thinking helps you develop better coping skills during the hard times of life. You learn to take one day at a time and this helps you to stay focused. I believe you are able to function better in life with a positive attitude. A negative attitude surely brings on stress and stress has been correlated with increased chances of developing cardiovascular disease which is the leading cause of death globally. It's not just outright or sudden death that you have to be afraid of. A negative attitude increases your chances of struggling with depression and anxiety.

A positive attitude makes it more likely that you will process psychologically sound choices and make healthy choices for your future. Positive thinking helps develop your psychological age so that it meets or exceeds your biological age. This means with positive thinking, it's not likely that you will be acting like a teenager at fifty years of age, at least not in an underdeveloped or inexperienced sense. You will carry yourself with more confidence as you look at the positive aspects of your current life status.

It is amazing, but our mind and the thoughts it houses can have an impact on our physical body, our health status, where we find ourselves in life, how long we live and how well or poorly we experience the journey of life.

People who have suffered the untimely loss of a loved one or other trauma often struggle with positive thinking. And they

46

have every right to do so for a period of mourning. However, if they continue to live in a world of grief, they actually stunt their psychological age to a noticeable degree. They are more prone to all of the undesirable consequences of negative thinking that have been mentioned. They will not be able to get past their memories of the trauma and struggle to move ahead in life with a negative outlook. If you can manage to trigger your sweet spot, it will enable you to transition past life's traumatic events more easily, but it is so difficult to accomplish this task when your thoughts are all negative.

A positive attitude makes it more likely that you will process psychologically sound choices and make healthy choices for your future.

Some people struggle with identifying the real issues behind the problems they encounter and blame themselves. They become negative as they don't separate themselves from the issue. They are unable to see the good in themselves or others.

Some people take disagreements with others personally and become defensive. This can occur from lack of self-confidence. We all need to take care not to take other people's opinions or suggestions personally. Learning to agree to disagree helps us to appreciate the thinking of others and nothing becomes personal.

There are others who anticipate the worst in every situation. They may be the ones going to work and upon discovering a flat tire, the entire day is ruined. They decide that because of the flat tire, the rest of the day is bad too. Or they wake up with a stomach ache and think they have cancer. They find it difficult to think that the stomach ache may be from the food they ate late last night.

Then there are others who might be how I used to be like. Everything was either good or bad, black or white. I used to be a perfectionist and every little thing would bother me: my personal life, the way I dressed, hygiene and grooming, and everything else. I would make negative comments about what I noticed about others and about what I saw in myself. As an example, I used to be very critical about the documents I produced for work. If I spelled a word wrong or used the wrong grammar, I would want to crucify myself. When I went shopping for flowers for Kathleen, I would assess each bunch to make sure I got the best. If I purchased something and saw a flaw, I would want to return it or fuss over why it was that I did not make the best choice. I would consider myself a failure if things did not go right. It was hard for me to see that it was okay to be less than perfect.

Here is another example of how negative thoughts can cripple your brain from thinking positively or looking for alternatives. Imagine you were walking down an alley and you saw a big, tall, strong guy coming towards you. Fear is registered in your mind and all you can think of is that he is coming to hurt you. Considering other alternatives goes out the window as you focus on seeing your life coming to an end, being raped, assaulted or robbed. The more the person draws close to you, the more fear cripples you and you cannot think of anything else.

When in a situation like this, where the person approaching is actually an assailant, most negative people freeze as fear and the worst outcome takes over their thoughts. They are unable to scream, run or fight back. Most people experience some degree of panic. The more dangerous a person looks, the more the mind becomes limited in processing what to do. However, those that think negatively find themselves even more paralyzed.

As I matured from perfectionism, I realized I don't have to be right all the time or always voice my opinion. I could allow others to make fools of themselves if it came to that, and give my opinion only if needed or asked. I changed my mindset and began to discover my sweet spot.

Creating new habits by changing my thought processes has helped me to live life in a more peaceful manner. My sweet spot helped create these habits in the sense that once you find the sweet spot, you will want to actively seek to maintain it. Finding your sweet spot can be a motivator for driving out poor habits like negative thinking.

People have to learn how to filter out negativity, to take compliments, to see the good in others and in life's situations, and to give credit where credit is due. Learning to be optimistic about life is crucial. You live with less stress and more power. You are able to walk away from an idea, a conversation or a decision without dwelling on the idea that you did something wrong.

Many people may find it more attractive to dismiss positive thinking as positive thinking appears to be for the simple-minded. Sometimes they might consciously or subconsciously feel there's not much to explore with positive thinking. This kind of thinking is more widespread than you might think. How many conversations have you been in where people were positive for over 90% of the conversation? How many even came close?

Choosing good things to be involved in can stimulate positive thoughts. Waking up in the morning and going to work is good because I am developing my career. Going to the gym and working out is good because I am developing my physical skills. Volunteering at a local community facility is good because I am contributing to others in society and gaining new skills. Having dinner with friends and family is good because I am developing my social skills. Going to church is good because I am building my spiritual life. Loving my spouse and children like there is no tomorrow is good because I am developing my ability to love and my relationships with others, and so on. Focusing on all the positive things I do helps me to see purpose for living which gives hope for a bright future.

FINDING YOUR SWEET SPOT

I may think of working and not be motivated to work. I may think of going to the gym and not be motivated, but I increase my chance of having positive thoughts because the overall impact of these activities is still positive. Focusing on things that are good to do and actually doing them makes a world of difference.

I had to learn how to refocus my thinking until it became a habit. Periodically during a conversation or during the day when I had some time to think about a conversation, I evaluated my thinking about the conversation and the person or people involved, especially if it was a conversation that was not peaceful or that did not settle well. I would reshape my thoughts around solutions. My main aim became putting a positive spin on the conversation or future conversations with the people involved.

Laughter drives out negativity. I have learned to smile and accept humour as a form of coping. I find laughing reduces my stress and keeps my spirit alive. I remember when I went for a job interview for a position in the area of mental health. The manager started off the interview with jokes in an attempt to create a light atmosphere. The jokes settled my nerves and at the same time brought out the funny side of my character. I remember the interviewer saying we all need a sense of humour when working in mental health, otherwise we would not survive. The higher the tension is, the greater the need for laughter. I think for the first fifteen to twenty minutes of the interview the interviewer tested my character by making me laugh, after which she did the formal interview. I guess my nerves went away completely. I did well and was hired. It was actually the best interview I have ever had.

Learning to surround yourself with people of the same positive nature is very important. Learn how to be with others who are positive and realize the importance of working to maintain good relationships with them. They are few in number, however, when they are in your life, you feel more free and comfortable to carry on a conversation. Talking with such people becomes an act of stress

50

relief since you can talk about any and everything without judgment or any negative motives. In conversation, you will find that you're not wasting time talking about others in a negative way or dwelling on any subject or people you are inclined to have negative feelings about.

Interestingly, the words we speak influence our mindset. Choosing your words carefully to avoid speaking negatively can change how you think, which in turn primes your brain to stimulate your sweet spot. For example:

- Instead of saying "I am too tired (or lazy) to go to the gym," say "I am not able to fit the gym in my schedule today but maybe tomorrow."
- Instead of saying "I am too busy," say "I am really occupied with some other errands, however we can look at it another day."
- Instead of saying "I can't do this as I have never done it before," say "Thanks for thinking of me. I can see this to be an opportunity to learn and grow."
- Instead of saying "It will not work," say "Let's see what options there are to adjust this so that it might work."
- Instead of saying "I can't help. I don't have the resources or tools for you," say "Let me see what I can do. Maybe I can do a bit of a research and will get back to you."
- Instead of saying "No one told me about it," say "I was not aware. Sorry I could not be there."

I am sure you get the idea.

Learning how to use words in a positive way can have a big impact on both the hearer and the speaker. Certain words bring joy and laughter. Others discourage, close doors and trigger anxiety. Negative words are so powerful that they can leave emotional scars. Positive words can be contagious and leave good memories.

FINDING YOUR SWEET SPOT

You will find that with a positive outlook, you see yourself saying "I can" instead of "I can't" more often. If you want to find your sweet spot, keep your brain happy by thinking positively. A brain that is happy has more positive effects than we can imagine. In addition to the many benefits I've mentioned, a positive outlook will make you feel more alert and energetic. You encounter fewer big obstacles, as the majority of your obstacles will be looked upon as opportunities. Mountains will become molehills. You will also command more respect from others. Your future will be bright if you will adopt a positive attitude.

Assess yourself and look at the ways in which you can become more positive. Some people are negative about their work, educational status, children, spouse, neighbours, church, and everything else under the sun. Learn how to live positively and see the light in every dark situation. Remember light is always on the other side of darkness.

When we have positive, happy thoughts we foster a sense of peace and internal joy. Negativity pollutes the brain while positivity cleans it.

QUESTIONS TO PONDER
1. What are the two forms of thinking that we have?
2. If positive thinking helps you develop better coping skills what does negative thinking do?
3. Choosing good things to be involved in can stimulate positive thoughts. Identify some activities that can help you with this.
4. How can laughter help dispel negativity?

avoiding
ADDICTION
to your thoughts

I thought of this chapter as I was driving home one day after work and was pondering on the love I have for my wife and children. I was thinking of the blessings I have and wondering what I did to acquire them. As I reflected on each of our children and my spouse, the thoughts became sweeter and sweeter, so much so that I did not want to stop thinking about each person and what they have contributed to my life.

Can we become addicted to our thoughts? Can our addictions cause us to live in a fantasy world? Can addiction to our thoughts ever be a good thing?

Firstly, let's look into what an addiction is. From my experience working with individuals with all forms of addictions, I can describe addiction as a habitual behaviour which consumes a person's life. It's like a stamp imprinted on the brain of the individual which creates a craving that can get out of one's control. When the individual's thoughts are settled around the addiction, the individual will make promises that they will never get involved in the addictive behaviour. However since addictions can be a coping mechanism for many, they fall time after time into engaging what they are addicted to.

FINDING YOUR SWEET SPOT

A person can be addicted to substances, emotions, sex, shopping, work, gambling and other fetishes that affect their mental health. When the addiction consumes the individual, it creates issues affecting a person's psychosocial life, medical and mental health. Some addictions lead to permanent mental illness.

I see addictions to be like cancer. If not controlled, it will eventually destroy a person's life and those who are part of their life. Addiction is being enslaved to something that can be quite challenging to the individual. People lose control over their cravings and would do anything to satisfy them. Some people have sold their bodies, stole from their loved ones and lost their jobs or family as a result of their addictions. Addictions hijack the brain and try to destroy it, as a cardiovascular issue damages the heart or tuberculosis destroys the lungs.

One of my colleagues, a psychiatrist, once explained to me that when the neurotransmitter dopamine is released in the nucleus accumbens it is registered in the brain. The addiction develops, and the more a person exposes their brain to the craving, the more the addiction develops. This is tied to the pleasure part of the brain and the individual who has an addiction finds that they cannot stop themselves.

Swallowing a pill, injecting an illicit drug, using alcohol, gambling, watching pornography, smoking, sniffing chemicals, and depending on the attention of others release a stronger dopamine signal than normal, which temporarily satisfies the craving in the mind of the person. The craving can be so overwhelming that the person will give up everything to be satisfied. The experience is like being stranded in a desert and finding yourself willing to do anything for a drink, even if it means drinking your own urine.

Having a better understanding of addictions will help you understand why I wanted to relate the concept to thought. I see thought addictions as having the power to strongly affect the emotional, physical and mental health of an individual. I call this

54

"the invisible addiction." This is the addiction that people don't see and no one is aware of unless they know the person in an intimate way and can read their body language.

This form of addiction doesn't involve using something physical or something that is visible to the naked eye. It's not a drug. It's not watching pornography. It's not spending money. It's not something you do physically. It is all in the mind.

I see thought addiction to be habitual thinking of a thought or a set of thoughts. It's like a fixation on something. I see it all the time with patients I work with as well as people in the community. Like the other more traditional forms of addictions I listed, it all starts with the first experience with the item or subject of addiction. It begins with the first drink, or the first bet, or the first use of marijuana or cocaine.

In the past, some have said addictions are caused by weak willpower, however, according to my psychiatrist colleagues, current studies show that it goes far beyond that.

Thought addictions start with a thought that a person keeps thinking over and over again. Negative thoughts might grow and develop hatred, discontentment or discord, causing damage in relationships. Innocent-seeming thoughts might become delusions or fantasies.

Thought addictions grow like a seed that is planted in the mind and usually they are negative, which affects one's thinking process. Sleeping patterns, eating habits and the ability to concentrate on anything else are affected. They might even have physical manifestations like headaches and muscle tension.

These types of thoughts reduce one's self-confidence, lower self-esteem, create paranoia, stir up past hurts, pull down self-images, reopen past emotional scars and kill joy and peace.

Surprisingly, the temporary high is not the main reason why someone depends on a thought addiction. Like other forms of addictions, most people develop an addictive pattern to cope with internal issues, numb their emotions, control their weaknesses or build courage. They develop stamina to face certain issues and sometimes partake in the addiction to quiet their noisy brain.

When I compare addictions, they all have similar purposes. Thought addictions have the same effect as alcohol, street drugs or gambling. They deplete people's minds which results in physical, mental and psychological effects on the well-being of a person.

Some people were told that they would never make it in life or called losers. They were told that they should be like their brother or sister or the next door neighbour. They were called stupid, crazy, lazy, uneducated, a bum, and the list goes on. This can play in the mind of that individual to the point where they start believing those words. They become addicted to the words so much that they actually see those words as applicable to them. It dominates their thoughts and affects their mind, their emotions, physical well-being and their future in general.

With counselling or psychotherapy and other forms of support, individuals can see the reality of the great impact negative words can have on occupying our foremost thoughts. Some clients have described the experience as like "a dark cloud being removed." Some clients have explained how they felt like a ton of bricks was taken off their shoulders or expressed how stupid they feel for believing lies. Shedding negative words and becoming free from the addictive thoughts they conjure up is like being given new skin and a new heart.

The realization is similar to a person who sobers up and becomes aware of all the negative words they said or the untoward behaviour they displayed when under the influence of whatever substance they used.

There is always the possibility for relapse, however with the right type of support and words of affirmation and encouragement, a person can move on to another level of their life and into maturity.

The scars that are left from thought addictions can be mended with psychotherapy, where the individual can learn to see the healed scar and walk away from it without stirring up the wound. They will be able to focus on the cause, the effects and the solutions for their own life. They will be able to see a bright future knowing that their past will not haunt them or try to pull them back into a dark world. They will become rooted in healthy thinking.

The cause of thought addictions will be dealt with from its roots in effective psychotherapy, where in time, the roots will be dissolved with no more power to grow or multiply. Whether it was caused by a trauma, negative words or other abuse, the possibility for healing is endless. Each cause will be viewed upon individually and dealt with accordingly.

The scars that are left from thought addictions
can be mended with psychotherapy,
where the individual can learn to
see the healed scar and walk away from it
without stirring up the wound.

Addictive thoughts fueled by negative words are just one form of addictive thoughts. Another form of thought addictions relates to relationships, which I find very fascinating. We may call it "falling in love." I look at it as another form of addiction. When couples find common ground, or even when people find new friends, it triggers the part of the brain that stimulates pleasure. You think of the people obsessively and can't wait to see them again or even to talk to them over the phone. They have done something to your mind and this is evident as you think of them throughout the day and the more you think of them the more you want to be with them.

Their name, appearance and actions flow through your thoughts from the moment you wake up to the time you go to sleep.

FINDING YOUR SWEET SPOT

Only a distraction could remove them from your thoughts. Other than that, you are constantly thinking about them. You dream about them and you often wonder what they are doing, and how they are doing. You think of all the things you would like to do when you meet again, the new places you will visit, the new dishes you will try, the fun activities you will do together and all the other things you want to experience with them.

Sometimes you might think about what you can do or say to make the other person laugh or smile. Or you envision their smile from previous interactions and dwell over the attraction you find in the person. You spend unwarranted amounts of time thinking about how "cute" the person is or how well they carry themselves. The thoughts can develop and lead to an addiction.

When the fantasy world crosses over into the real world and we become out of touch with reality, then addiction has taken over and is leading to a fixation, which could lead to stalking in some cases. Our brains were not made to stay stuck in one mode. It can affect our mental health and even our ability to function normally.

A good rule to remember is that you will always be you and the person will always be his or herself. Having fun and spending time together is all okay. Plan activities with the person and write them down, but keep your thoughts moving ahead. Never allow your thoughts to overtake your mind.

Don't be fooled. Just because your thoughts might surround something that seems positive does not mean that they are always healthy. Although the addictive thoughts revolve around the love you have for a person, it can stimulate negative emotions. Some people become anxious, sad, desperate, jealous, worried, scared and concerned unnecessarily because of thought addiction. Most of us can control our emotions, however there are times when our emotions get a hold of us and hijack our thinking process.

If the person is running late, the phone died, or they are unable to make contact with us, we start thinking of the worst scenarios because of the obsession we have developed from thinking about the person too much.

You may have issues parting with a person. You find it's difficult to say goodbye and you live in the same town, for instance. Something is wrong and it probably has too much addictive thinking at the root. You know the pleasure (or high) will go away if the person leaves and you want to do everything in your power to stay with them as long as you can.

You soon realize that this person is taking up more and more of your time—both time with them and time in thought thinking about them. You find them to be more important than your friends, yourself, your family members, your beliefs and other important parts of your life.

The pleasure found in addictive thoughts can mimic the triggering of the sweet spot in your brain but they are two different things. Sweet spot pleasure is sweeter and lasts longer. Addictive pleasure is never truly satisfied.

Some clients have explained that their brain responds only to so much thinking before it shuts down. Working in the field, my personal observation is that eventually the brain adapts to the thoughts and the addiction is no longer as pleasurable. The addiction about a particular person or subject either changes or fades away until another thought arises that does the same. This may take three weeks or a month when the cycle starts all over again.

The reason why people can get carried away with music is for the same reason. The music triggers the memory of the thoughts that were being recited in the brain about the things they love and it stimulates the mind. It can keep a person happy, however when the music is over and the person leaves the environment the feelings go away.

According to a psychiatrist colleague, dopamine interacts with glutamate, which is another neurotransmitter. Glutamate supports the brain's system of reward learning which supports the basic needs of human existence such as exercise, play, sex, food and sleep. This interaction can lead to a healthy thought life if facilitated properly. Living in the real world, healthy thought fixations that resemble addictions can lead an individual to find their sweet spot.

I remember when I was in university, I was doing a course on the brain and the teacher shared about two areas of the brain. He explained the hippocampus is like the hippo which is territorial and the amygdala is like the armadillo which comes out at night to feed and has memory of its feeding ground. Both the hippocampus and the amygdala store environmental cues that are associated with whatever stimulates pleasure in the brain. This conditions the brain for its craving whenever a person is in the environment that will trigger memory of the stimulant.

Don't allow your thoughts to have a life of their own. Learn to stop and assess yourself and ask the question, "Why am I thinking along this line?" Ask what happened in the past that is making you feel the way you are feeling? Do what you can to pull yourself away from yielding to those thoughts.

Gaining knowledge of your addictive thoughts is the next step to priming the mind to discover your sweet spot and explore happiness that is lasting. Learn to stop yourself and consider how foolish your thoughts are and how they might be causing your emotions to be like a roller coaster. Step back from your thinking and your addictive thoughts will subside.

In the next chapter I want to focus on feelings. It's our emotions which are stimulated by our thoughts. Some feelings are expressed through triggers of incidents that have been witnessed and stored in the brain, which can be positive or negative. Positive events will bring a sense of joy and contentment, whereas negative thoughts bring about sadness and discomfort. These can swing us in opposite directions, to or away from our sweet spot.

QUESTIONS TO PONDER

1. There are many things we can become addicted to. Name some of the common ones. Where can the path of addiction lead you?
2. Explain what thought addictions are. Does thought addiction have the same effect as alcohol, street drugs or gambling?
3. What are some of the causes of thought addiction?
4. What are some negative emotions thought addiction can stimulate?

focusing
FEELINGS on

The parts of the brain have counterparts in our emotional worlds. There are people who don't have a brain injury per se, but live like they do. Their "emotional lobes" have been affected. For instance, when the temporal lobe has been affected, a person feels they have lost their sense of humour. They have difficulty enjoying life as though they have lost all "smell, taste and sound" for life.

I would like to suggest if someone does feel like their emotional frontal lobe has been affected from a past experience, it may relate to a psychological trauma, relationship issues, being bullied, or other drawbacks. However you don't have to live with it. We can either allow our negative experiences to steal our happiness or we can look at all possible solutions in order to be set free. Freedom will help us to find our sweet spot allowing us to bring a twist in our emotional vision to focus on positivity and prosperity. When I see clients prosper in all that they do, their family life, relationship with their spouse, family, children, community, colleagues and neighbours, they live in that freedom of being a conqueror over life's issues. They live in their sweet spot.

Although there are circumstances that may come our way in life, we have to learn how to find solutions, rather than allow them to pull us down. Allowing our brain to problem-solve and find the solutions that can help us move ahead can be negated by some people, as they find it more comforting to wallow in the "muck of life." We should never lose touch with the smell, taste or sound of life. The emotional brain can find alternatives to draw us to our sweet spot.

We need to learn how to smell the freshness of all possibilities and pursue the ability to capture the smells of life. No one should ever feel that they can no longer enjoy the smell of success, prosperity, happiness, purpose, excitement or love. We need to make all attempts to capture the scent of life and enjoy its fragrance.

We should not be afraid to taste life either. Until we make attempts to go beyond our own boundaries, remove our limitations and extend ourselves we will never know what we can and cannot do. We can be cheating ourselves from finding the sweet spot. Like with the diamond on your ring, only if it is real will it indicate to the tester when the light changes to green. Are we giving our brain a chance to see what it can do?

When we listen to the heartbeat of our emotions we can be driven towards the sweet spot in our brain. Paying as much attention to our emotional lobes as we should to our brain will put us one step closer.

Try to think of your emotional short-term memory like those writing pads children use that have a plastic film over them. You can write on one and once you lift the film up, the writing or drawing disappears. Some of us want to live like this writing pad and have all the negative issues of life and stressors go away. Unfortunately, we need to work at them and find solutions.

Remember the part of the brain associated with taste, touch and temperature? We need to learn how to be connected with ourselves and others through taste, touch and temperature. So many times we get out of touch with reality and live in a fantasy world. We lose our sense of what it means to be cold or hot as we are content in where we are in life. We are happy for others who are progressing but cannot see it for ourselves.

64

It's like going to a sports game. We are happy for the players, even if they lose the game, but we cannot see ourselves playing. We need to learn how to taste, and touch our reality and feel the temperature associated with it.

This may mean moving around, looking for what makes us happy and indulging ourselves in it. No need to procrastinate and allow the opportunity to pass by. It may never come again. We need to live in a real world, not in a psychotic world where we are out of touch with reality.

There are many of us who live in a delusional life or hallucinate with false hopes. Unless we push ourselves to reality we will never know the joy of living in the sweet spot.

Let's consider our emotional frontal lobe. How many of us have been stuck in the same place for years and find there is no movement in our life? In fact, I have clients whose family members would say that "All they do is work, go home, work, go home." They feel that they "have no life."

We all need to have some movement in our lives. When I was growing up, my mother used to say "Stagnant water has no life." When water is stagnant it begins to stink and nothing can live in it. Eventually the water will dry up. We all need to have wells of water inside our lives to keep us young at heart.

Movement is a change of position, change of attitude, change of personality and character. It will change how we view life with expectations to excel. Our emotional movement will help us draw closer to the sweet spot where we can live in peace.

In order for us to move ahead, we all need to take advantage of time through planning, organizing and learning how to problem-solve. Some of us have difficulty in doing this and fail to move ahead in life. We prefer for someone else to do it all for us. We can only draw closer to our sweet spot when we can plan our lives with short-term, long-term and miracle goals. These goals will then need to be taken to another level where we organize them so they can be accomplished. Problem-solving is learning to deal with each obstacle that comes our way that might prevent our goals from being accomplished.

We can only draw closer to our sweet spot when we can plan our lives with short-term, long-term and miracle goals.

Remember the occipital lobe and its role in processing images? You can only imagine how many people are psychologically blind and are unable to see what they have that is of value. They are always looking at what others have and are blinded to the gifts they have in their possession. Some of us need to analyze what we do have and show appreciation rather than turn a blind eye to it. Having emotional blindness can prevent us from finding our sweet spot in the brain.

As mentioned earlier, our (true) emotions are part of the frontal lobe where the executive function resides. Every emotion has a purpose and when the brain is affected, the emotions of a person can be difficult to produce or manufacture. The emotions are what you and I feel which, at times, can seem to interfere with our thinking. However, emotions aid in our ability to express ourselves.

Our emotions give information to the world around us and they motivate how we behave. When we learn how to recognize our feelings and the benefits they carry, we are able to understand how they affect our ability to function. The executive function will be able to alter your response to every situation you face in life.

Your environment plays a big part in how the brain is triggered through emotion. You wouldn't play heavy metal at a funeral or sing hymns at a nightclub. The brain is programmed to adjust the emotions to the environment. Certain environments will create bursts of energy whereas other environments make your feel lethargic, tired and restless.

Our very thoughts affect our emotions which send signals to the brain. When we feel anxious a signal is released to the brain and we start to sweat. Our hands become cold or clammy. Our heart rates elevate and it may feel like a ton of bricks has been stacked on our chest.

We cry, laugh, become angry, get upset and get happy all through the brain. I am amazed how much information our brain has to process every day subconsciously. This is one reason I encourage clients to learn how to meditate on a word or sentence to give their brain a rest. When the brain is overworked it affects our thought processes.

Focusing on our feelings helps us from succumbing to other negative emotions. Let's use sadness as an example. When we are in touch with how we feel, we are equipped to accept what the cause of the sadness is and realign our goals to move ahead. We become cautious and alert. There is a need to reflect on our feelings. Anxiety, depression and anger may manifest themselves when our feelings are not adding to our thought process.

When we focus on our feelings, it helps us to make better decisions in our life. If we focus on what we think instead of how we feel we may not make the right decision, since our feelings help us to identify our strengths.

Anger is a reaction to what we feel, however it develops from being frustrated or overwhelmed by life's stressors or trauma which are locked inside the emotional realm. When the opportune time comes, anger gains its freedom and until is it treated, it will take every opportunity to express itself. It stirs up the emotional brain.

Another emotion we see regularly is pride. We all have some form of pride, whether we express it or not. The positive aspect of pride builds your self-esteem. The negative aspects of pride make you feel that you are better than everyone else.

Guilt is another feeling. We often see this one with the couples we counsel. Guilt can stem from the feeling of being remorseful after committing a "crime" or breaking "the rule" of fidelity. Guilt affects the brain and individuals have the choice to express their feelings of guilt or cover them up. Guilt helps people to understand that they were wrong in the choice they made.

Happiness is one of my favorite feelings. Happiness can cause one to cry with tears of joy or laugh, stirring up all the positive emotions in one's heart. It can become contagious and opens the doors for you to move ahead in life. It will brighten your day, help you to think clearly and maintain a positive lifestyle.

Looking at a person who is fearful can lead to feeling defeated. When a person recognizes fear, they can protect themselves from assaults, hurts, animal attacks and being in the wrong place with the wrong people but they can also be so scared that they become unable to protect themselves. But then there is the fear of those in authority where you are in awe to be in the presence of a king, president, prime minister, or even God. This is considered good fear, appreciating what is given to you, which can be quite humbling.

Some people have not learned how to get in touch with their emotions, and find it difficult to express feelings. They avoid or guard themselves from being able to share their feelings. Emotions can be a learned behaviour which children access from their parents. If emotions were not expressed while you were growing up, the chances are that you may not see the need or the importance to express your emotions.

Some people express their feelings at a major crisis when they are stuck and not sure what else to do. Their emotions are expressed and they themselves are unaware of their own feelings. The brain needs an avenue to vent and it uses our emotions.

Vulnerability is a door which can be opened for feelings to be seen and expressed. Some people may view it as weak, while others use it to gain sympathy and support. Some people may have been hurt while in the stage of being vulnerable and have prohibited themselves from opening that door again. They may be fearful of exposing their hurts or embarrassed and refuse to allow themselves to share their feelings.

We need to learn how to stop ourselves, take a few deep breaths, slow the brain down and reflect on our feelings. People have difficulty doing this and this can eventually lead to their lives being scarred from feelings.

We can create synapses between our prefrontal lobe and our limbic system when we face our emotions. I try to explain this to our clients when we share about the importance of sharing feelings and expressing emotions. Our limbic system is a part of the brain that specializes in feelings, which helps us to focus and meditate when leveraged correctly. Our minds mature and grow when synapses are created. This helps us to stay focused in life.

We can count discomfort as one of our feelings. What do we do when we feel discomfort? Most people will try whatever it takes to make themselves comfortable. There may be times when we cannot figure out the root cause of why we feel the way we do since there are so many reasons that can bring discomfort. It may not always be as simple as a pebble in your shoes or a rock-hard pillow. Depending on the level of discomfort, you can easily be stressed out which can cause anxiety or anger to rise. The key is to recognize how you feel and then to problem-solve.

Hurt is another feeling. No one would choose to ignore the pain of a cut or of a sore body part. We try to find some form of solution, especially if the pain is lasting longer than anticipated. We don't ignore how we feel, but identify where it hurts and try to find a solution depending on the cause of the hurt.

Disappointment is also a feeling that we experience. We can feel disappointed at ourselves or people we trust and believe in, even our own family members. We can be disappointed if we did not get the job, or pass the exam, or receive negative comments or actions taken by someone we trust. We get disappointed when the service we are being provided with, the vacation we invested our money in, the music CD we purchased, the vehicle we invested in, the course or workshop we attended, or the gifts we received for our birthday don't satisfy us. Learning to recognize that it's okay to be disappointed and to express how we feel in a mature way speaks volumes. Also the way you choose to work towards a solution shows your maturity level.

I have clients share their frustrations with me. They are given a time frame to vent and get it off their chest. Expressing the frustration you encounter is healthy, once it is done in a safe environment without hurting yourself or anyone else. It's good to get the frustration off your chest and explore the cause with the goal of finding a solution. This again will carry you further in life. You will learn from your mistakes and discover what to avoid in the future to reduce your level of frustration. This is a feeling that you should express. If it is kept inside, you will eventually become like a volcano and erupt. And depending on where and with whom you choose to express your frustration, you may end up having a psychiatric assessment. Frustration gives a clear indication that your expectation is not being met.

I have several clients who express that they feel inadequate, a feeling of being unworthy without cause. This feeling usually makes you think you are not talented, skilled or experienced to get the job done. Usually, this feeling stems from a lack of confidence and low self-esteem. I believe we can do all that is reasonable and rational that we put our minds to. We need to be determined and stay focused. Learning to acquire knowledge from others and to use what you learn to your advantage will carry you through. Look for the positive in every negative.

Another feeling that we see more and more today is loneliness. We see this with singles, single parents, children who are unable to engage with others, professionals, people in positions of power and others. There are so many lonely people. I have taken calls at crisis centers and people call all hours of the day and the night to chat. They despise being alone and at times feel like life is not worth living. Chatting on the phone helps build them up to move on to another day. We need to validate loneliness and know that it's okay to feel lonely. Finding a solution to work with your loneliness is important. Joining clubs, centers, utilizing distress lines, engaging with family and friends or working on a hobby can help loneliness. When I was single, it was very difficult to be alone, sleep alone, cook alone, grocery shop alone and so on. But I learned how to keep myself busy with others as well as when I was alone. Some people may feel loneliness is the need for sex, but it is not. We are creatures who need to communicate with something or someone and when that's not the case we feel empty. Some like to be alone and have time to process their lives. This is very healthy. I call it "me time."

There is a long list of feelings we can go through one by one, but I believe you are getting the picture of learning to identify your feelings and work toward progression. Each feeling has the potential to affect you in a negative or a positive way. Negative and positive emotions are created in us for a purpose. We need to explore the reasons behind them and decide which emotions are healthy and which are unhealthy. Most people would choose to be happy and stay positive but that may not always be possible due to one's circumstances.

Negative feelings help us to identify challenges and threats that come up in life. We need to learn how to walk on egg shells when needed or walk away when danger approaches. We become more aware of the world we live in when we can identify the negative feelings, which in turn help us to survive. We are able to get to the core of the problem when we identify what is causing us to feel negative and can work on a solution.

FINDING YOUR SWEET SPOT

Regardless of how we feel, we need to have a balance in our emotion. Some people are emotionally driven while others express little to no emotions. Having a balance in our feelings will keep us stabilized and strong. We will not be looking for triggers to stimulate our emotions, but if they come we will be passionate about our feelings.

Positive feelings balance the negative feelings, which help us to become more alert and aware. Positive feelings affect our brain where they pull our attention towards making decisions that are rational and make sense in the context of the knowledge and skills we have.

Our memory is triggered by positive feelings which bring ideas together to resolve issues and plan solutions to the roadblocks we encounter. We are able to make choices that are best for ourselves that bring a sense of satisfaction. We become more open to new adventures, new possibilities, new challenges and new growth. We look at correction and discipline as a way of growth rather than the opposite.

I have taught clients that learning to have a positive attitude in life and living with positive feelings will lead to a healthier, happier, hope-filled life. You will be able to get along with most people, find it easier to accept changes, become more flexible, and enjoy the challenges that come across your path.

The clients we see have been able to build their resilience through positive feelings, as it opens their minds to look for means of coping and ways of solving issues. Through retraining the brain, we have been able to see clients' attitudes change to become more positive as a result of learning to live life with a focus on positive feelings.

When we feel good about ourselves we can progress in life and do more for ourselves and those we work with. We find joy in serving others. We dress better, care for ourselves in a more detailed way, eat healthier, treat others better and carry a different vibe than those living with a focus on negative feelings.

When negative feelings are manifesting themselves and you are aware that they will lead to destruction through your behaviour, you must turn your negatives into positives, or control your negatives.

There are several keys to controlling negative behaviour. The first key to take control of your negative feelings which may lead you to say or make an obstacle of yourself is to stop. Learn to stop what you are saying, thinking and acting out. Walk away if need be. Learn to divert yourself and bring yourself to silence.

Secondly, drop all the things that you were engaged in before you got into the negative world. Drop the thought, drop your actions, and drop your solutions. In this part of the process most people are unable to think clearly and say things they regret or act in ways that may not be appropriate. Unless the negative feelings are beneficial, you have to drop what is causing them to grow.

And thirdly, roll. Don't physically roll (although this may help some people), but roll out all that caused you to enter into the negative world. Roll out the cause of the issue, the cause of the thought and the cause of your feelings. Remember 5W 1H.

1. Why are you feeling the way you are?
2. What is causing you to feel this way?
3. When did the feelings start?
4. Who is responsible for the feelings?
5. Where did these feelings stem from?
6. How can I deal with them?

It is important to identify the emotions that are being formulated as a result of your feelings. If you can manage your emotions you can control your feelings. I have encouraged clients to consider different therapeutic methods to control their feelings and manage their emotions. Later on in this book I will list some of the therapies that seemed to work with those struggling in this area.

FINDING YOUR SWEET SPOT

In the next chapter, I would like to share about feeding the brain. I believe it is very important to feed the brain food that will assist us in finding our sweet spot. Therapies are great as diversions, however, to help the brain function in a healthy capacity we need brain food.

QUESTIONS TO PONDER

1. We all need to have some movement in our lives. What is movement and how does it draw us closer to the sweet spot in our brain?
2. Why is it important to learn to identify your feelings and work toward progression? Name some of these feelings.
3. We need to have a balance in our emotions and our feelings. Explain how that is possible.
4. What are the three keys to controlling negative behaviour?

feeding
THE
brain

There is a delicate balance that must be achieved—a balance between not having too many thoughts but also not leaving your mind under-stimulated. The trick is to keep the brain occupied but focused or as I like to put it, "well fed." In putting together this chapter, I thought of a hungry child, who screams and cries to express his hunger. The brain also cries out for food in a number of ways.

Have you ever wondered why when we were children we didn't worry and weren't bombarded with thoughts as we are today? I cannot recall spending time worrying about much or becoming anxious as a child. When I was about fourteen years old, exams were about the only things that were a worry for me. At seventeen years old when I starting to think about relationships, I had thoughts surrounding what it would be like to have a mate.

I am aware not everyone was like me. Some may have been abused, lived on the street, lived with a single parent, lived with an alcohol-addicted parent, were exposed to illicit drugs at an early age or the like. I am aware of this and I am sure the brain started to become noisier earlier as they were forced to grow up early. Unless we make efforts to counteract noise, it will always be true that the more responsibility we have, the more noise our brains make.

FINDING YOUR SWEET SPOT

What can we do to reduce unnecessary thoughts? How exactly do you take control of your thoughts before your life and thoughts become disordered or you cross the fantasy line and you become out of touch with reality? We can feed the brain!

Not just any food will do. The brain needs to be fed the right food in order to reduce the noise. The wrong food can cause the brain to think more. An overly stimulated brain will have difficulty settling down.

The brain needs to be fed the right food in order to reduce the noise. The wrong food can cause the brain to think more.

Put yourself in a child's shoes and think of all the things they do that quiet their brain. As children, our minds were occupied with fun, outdoor activities (fishing, climbing trees, planting things) and creating things. I used to bike, draw, play hide and seek, and play board games. Children today are focused primarily on schoolwork, chatting with their friends, texting and gaming. Although these may be helpful, children need age-appropriate stimulants to divert noisy thoughts and dwelling on adult issues and so do adults.

I would like to devote a large part of this chapter to providing specific ideas of what you can do to feed your brain. Here are some ways to help quiet your brain that have been very beneficial to some of the clients I work with.

1. Develop a daily routine and plan for the day, week and year. Planning feeds the brain information so that you will not need to worry what the day will be like. You know exactly what to expect and it will put your mind at ease.

2. Set goals that are short-term goals, goals that are long-term goals, and miracle goals. This will give your brain some form of comfort that you are working towards something that will be

beneficial. Vacation plans, addressing your hobbies, plans to connect with people, bills to pay and appointments are all scheduled and structured.

3. Read a book. This activity feeds the brain more than you can imagine. Instead of your brain looking for solutions for the magnified problems in your life, it stays focused as you read and join in on the journey of the book.

4. Watch a movie, especially with others. Watching movies can be fun and exciting depending on the movie. Movies can stimulate the brain in a negative or positive way, but they definitely keep you focused. Watching sports does the same. Your brain stays focused as you feed it with stimulants from the game you're watching. Your brain will not be focusing on other things if the movie or the game is interesting or exciting.

5. Play board games or electronic games. These also feed the brain. You are focused on trying to win or complete each level. You need to be careful though, as gaming can lead to an addiction. You need to be mindful of the amount of time you spend on games.

6. Text, email, browse the internet or chat over the phone. Technology can be a great tool to stimulate the brain. Some people have difficulty letting go of their phone as they "need" to text or call someone constantly. While this is a distraction, some level of interaction with these technologies can be healthy.

7. Learn to be curious about life, the people and the things you come across. This forces your brain to think but not in a worrisome way. Asking why things work the way it do is healthy. You will step into research mode and you will narrow down your thoughts to think on one thing.

8. Eat well. When you eat well you can't criticize yourself for the junk food or the fact that you are gaining weight. You are proud of your wise food choices. You're not down on yourself and

you have no need to compare yourself to others. When you are health conscious, you convince your brain that you are okay and there is no need to worry about weight or what others think. Healthy eating brings good energy into your body and mind.

Good food will also give your body the nutrients it needs to support your brain. As a child my mother used to say we need brain food and would make sure we had fish during the week and fish oil every morning. It had an awful aftertaste that lingered the entire morning. Nuts, seeds, coconut oil, blueberries, milk, eggs, meats, turmeric, fruits and vegetables were all considered healthy for the brain and must-haves while in school. Even though my parents were not exposed to the nutritional knowledge of these foods we see being promoted today, their parents knew what was good for them. I still joke with our children about using coconut oil and goat milk. My mom used to put so much coconut oil on my body and on my head, that I would go to school with the oil running down my neck. We used to drink goat's milk from freshly milked goats and we had lots of turmeric with rice. Nothing has changed. These are all still healthy for growth and development.

9. Exercise regularly. Make a conscious effort to walk around the block every day. Walk up some stairs or visit the gym. The effort of exercising convinces your brain that you are caring for yourself. A guy at the gym once told me that exercise increases your brain function as well. It is believed that it causes brain cells to grow as exercise is associated with neurogenesis.

10. Take on a new task, new challenge or new responsibility. This will keep you focused on things that will enhance your ability to stay focused. A simple task like building a fish pond in the backyard, painting your kitchen or bedroom, or washing your car can be just what you need to stay focussed.

11. Think positively. Positive thinking causes the brain to be more alert and reduces stress and anxiety. Working with the

community has taught me a lesson in life: positive thinking will help build a good reputation. You will be considered a trustworthy person who will attract others when you think positively. You carry a different form of energy which is attractive to others. You live with a smile on your face knowing there is good in every bad situation.

12. Take care of yourself: body, soul and spirit. This will help you feel better about who you are. It will build your self-esteem and confidence.

13. Listen to music. Music therapy is an excellent way to feed the brain. In fact when I was in school doing a course on the brain, I learned that music positively stimulates the brain, especially classical music. I remember my wife sharing with me a discussion she had with our younger daughter who was about eleven years old at the time. My wife was driving home after picking our daughter up from an activity and had classical music on. Our daughter commented that she was enjoying the music. My wife asked, "why?" She replied, "It makes me feel smart." You can read more about music therapy in my book entitled *Music Therapy and Mental Illness*.

14. Write down your thoughts before bed. This keeps the brain calm. It convinces the brain that you will not forget your thoughts and the brain settles. Keep a pad of paper or a journal with a pen handy beside your bed. This will put your mind at ease and help you get a good night's sleep.

15. Socialize. Talking to and spending time with others is an important type of food your brain needs in order to stay alert. You have to think when talking to people. Developing relationships, working with people and connecting with others are all healthy.

16. Challenge yourself. I see people doing puzzles, adult app games, reasoning games, memory games and other mind-training activities. This is a good practice.

17. Take time to analyze your body parts. This is very important for the brain. It has to send messages to all parts of your body and therefore, spending some time on a regular basis to notice your body is very good for the brain. The brain can develop images which will be stored in the mind. This is good food for the future when body parts stop working.

18. Look for new ways to learn new things. It's good to challenge the brain. Work out at the gym. Learn to swim if you've never done so before. Try your hand at a new language, hobby or craft. New activities cater to the plasticity of your brain.

There are ways of tricking the brain to foster new thoughts that are simple yet have shown to be effective for those who have applied them. You can add to this list as you go through it:

1. Exchange the shoes that you would normally wear with that certain pant, skirt or dress with another pair.
2. Change the colour of some of your clothing or shoes to a colour you are not used to wearing.
3. Sit at a different seat at church, work or even in your home, especially if you are like us with seven children who all like sitting in the same seat.
4. Try new foods and drinks
5. Open the car window and feel the breeze when driving. Learn to use your five senses when doing this (hearing, smelling, tasting, touching and seeing). Implement your senses and see what happens.
6. Throw a ball, run or even jump.
7. Hug a tree.
8. Count your pocket change and look at the year each coin was printed.
9. Look at something from a different angle. Turn a picture or a cup upside down and examine it.
10. Climb a tree and look down.
11. Write a poem or a song, even a short story.

12. Paint a picture or make an attempt to draw something.

13. Switch around your morning routine.

14. Identify how many objects and foods in a room have the same colour, shape or size.

15. Go to a store or supermarket and look how things are organized and imagine how you would do it better. Justify why you would make each choice to switch things around.

16. Try a certain food item in different recipes and forms of cooking. For example, experiment with chicken or potatoes. See how many ways they can be cooked.

17. Try a different way of developing your spiritual life. Look at what can you do differently. Maybe pray for fifteen minutes longer, create a prayer list, appoint someone in your family to lead prayer every night, read your Bible from Genesis to Revelation, or attempt to read the Old and New Testaments at the same time. Be creative.

18. Listen to music you would not normally listen to, maybe in a different language.

19. Learn to laugh.

20. Learn to sing.

21. Learn to cry.

22. Go to bed earlier than your normal sleep time and wake up earlier.

23. Try to eavesdrop on someone else's conversation.

24. Pay attention to details about a room, a car or a house.

25. Change your closets from time to time. Rearrange your clothes.

26. Rearrange your home, room by room, including your bedroom.

27. Start a project or a hobby.

28. Do something kind for someone.

29. Program yourself to say hi to ten people per day, per week, for four weeks.

When considering what to do, age should never be an obstacle. Trying new things and launching out into new adventures keep the brain happy and give the soul purpose for living. I was reading an article one day about Smoky Dawson who was ninety-two years old when he did his first album "Homestead of My Dreams," Dorothy Davenhill Hirsch was eighty-nine years old when she visited the North Pole. Kimani Maruge was eighty-four years old when he started the first grade. Mohr Keet was ninety-six years old when he went bungee jumping. Alice Porlock of Great Britain published her first book, *Portrait of My Victorian Youth*, when she was one hundred two years old. Nola Ochs became the oldest person to receive a college diploma, a degree in general studies with an emphasis on history. There are many people who can attest to the value of new adventures at any age.

The brain is stimulated and becomes excited. With new adventures, it's like going on trips where there's lots to do and discover regularly. Your capacity to store memories increases.

There are lots of things we can do to help our brains grow and develop in healthy ways, however, we seldom practice them. **This is certainly one reason why we are not functioning on the level we should be.** Feeding your brain is a work in progress, but the result is rewarding: a happy brain, happy feelings, and a happy life.

Be adventurous and pursue all happiness to keep your youth alive. Learn to dance in the rain and run in the mud. Plan your life to live it to its fullest and explore what this world has to offer. Whatever it is you do, it has to become a daily habit.

Before this chapter, when you thought of brain food, I am sure you thought that it referred to healthy foods you need to eat in order to have your brain function well. Now you know that while that is a part of it, your brain also needs food in the form of new, attention-grabbing and challenging activities that will allow it to focus and assist it in its development. Such activities increase your capacity for memory, keep the mind alert, sharpen your thinking abilities and prime the mind for you to find your sweet spot and experience that release of chemicals that brings a feeling of true joy.

QUESTIONS TO PONDER

1. What can we do to control unnecessary thoughts?
2. When thinking back to when you were a child what are some things you remember you did that quieted your brain? How would it be different if you were a child growing up today?
3. Can you name some activities you have used in the past or present that have helped you feed your brain?
4. What have you learned in this chapter that you can apply to your own personal life?

find what
YOU love

I did not figure out what I was really good at until I started to work in the area of mental health. I started to work in the community as a support worker in a group home in 1990 and then began to work with acquired brain injury clients. I was only at the surface of something amazing that would bring deep contentment. This was when the sweet spot was first triggered but not fully excited.

I was always fascinated by the brain yet did not find the sweet spot until I discovered the compassion I had towards those struggling with mental illness. I knew I was born for this. It was not a job but a hobby.

There are many moments when my sweet spot came alive, triggering happy chemicals. These came from moments of reflecting on accomplishments, progress and successes, and moments of purpose and fulfillment. Each has a story leading to a happy sensation.

I first discovered my first sweet spot when I found my wife Kathleen. It's not just the falling in love that has stimulated my sweet spot with Kathleen. It's the staying in love. The moment I fell in love with Kathleen, I knew I was taking on the responsibility of staying in love and making the relationship work. There were many occasions in our early years of marriage when we went through the valley of struggles. As we worked on maintaining a healthy relationship and resolving the issues that came our way, the sweet spot kept its fire. Sometimes it felt like there was only a bit of warmth and the fire was dying, however, when we worked on our lives together and individually, the fire grew bigger.

Kathleen brought out emotions I thought never existed, and a joy that has been unspeakable. There have been many struggles that could have affected our relationship, however, we worked on the issues and kept focused on our future together. Up until this day, we do the same. Many people have asked us, "When did you two become one?" I say after about twenty years of marriage. This is when we stepped up to another level of our relationship. All along we had a good relationship, however, after about twenty years, we reached a place where our love had grown to be like that of "Romeo and Juliet." We still have differences of opinion, and see situations from different angles, however we never allow issues or problems to stand between us.

When the children came along, the sweet spot created another burst of sweet joy. A different form of joy came to my heart and awakened areas in my life I never knew I had. The sweet spot just kept getting sweeter as our seven children grew and as we experience each level of their maturity.

Education was an accomplishment that brought about sweetness. It triggered the sweet spot when I started to learn about different areas of life that I never knew existed. I learned to understand people, the reason for people's behaviour and the science behind the life of every living person.

One point I stress with our children is the difference between employment and a career. Most people have jobs that are paying the bills, but not necessarily jobs they want to be in. They work just to survive and that job can be changed anytime. My first job in Canada was working on a farm. I worked with tobacco and mushrooms crops. Then I worked as a drywall taper. During this period I also worked in a group home. Later on, I worked as a leisure buddy with men who had acquired brain injuries. I worked as a photo technician (big name but minimum wage at $5.25 an hour). I worked and participated in several humanitarian aid programs—some paid and some unpaid—until I went back to school and started to work on my career. Upon completing school I received four job offers in four different fields of work: correction services with men who were in a halfway house, work for the city, work for children's welfare and work in mental health. I started my career in mental health and never looked back. It was the best choice I made.

Another area where my sweet spot was awakened was in finding out that I could actually have fun exercising and staying fit. Everyone should have some "me time." Some people enjoy shopping, some enjoy fishing.

Whatever it is, it is very important to have alone time and enjoy what you like. I found going to the gym to be one of my favorite things to do alone on a regular basis.

I also enjoy travelling outside of the country three to four times a year. I like doing missions, public speaking, helping the impoverished, having family time and doing research when I travel.

Whatever you like to do, pursue it! These are areas that keep the sweet spot in the brain stimulated. I look forward to these events as they are planned a year or two in advance. As I make time for them, my sweet spot comes alive and I am able to function more effectively.

When we can permanently keep the sweet spot
in the brain stimulated with events and activities that are
legal, transparent and morally acceptable we enjoy the
great pleasure that comes with them.

I believe when individuals are able to enjoy what they do and feel compensated for their busy life, their sweet spot is awakened. But this involves enjoying *wisely*. Some people have relied on unhealthy behaviours to quicken their sweet spot like clubbing, the bar scene, sexual encounters with strangers, escorting or prostituting themselves, and addictive behaviours (doing drugs, drinking, gambling, pornography, eating). However, the joy found in these activities is only momentary and does not have the same effects as when your sweet spot is stimulated in a sustainable way. When we can permanently keep the sweet spot in the brain stimulated with events and activities that are legal, transparent and morally acceptable we enjoy the great pleasure that comes with them.

Some people enjoy the edgy side of life and seek thrills like bungee jumping, skydiving, amusement park rides, eating in the dark, "fear factors" (eating worms, having snakes crawl over them, watching sharks close up from inside a cage, etc.). Again these are good for the moment but do not last a long time. We have a need to stimulate the sweet spot and are capable of doing anything to make that happen, but don't get caught up searching in wild and destructive places for your pleasure.

I have heard of a sex trade, where people spend thousands of dollars to have sex with a young boy or girl without their consent. Many people harbor sexual fetishes and curiosities that can pull them into new worlds. It becomes like an addiction once they have a taste and they want more—until it destroys them. Many people risk their marriages with sexual, emotional affairs and other exotic and addictive pursuits.

Although unhealthy thrills give power to the individual, and a small taste of what the sweet spot can do, they are like mirages that never bring true satisfaction.

When it comes down to it, people like to have a sense of certainty. They want to feel loved and connected, they want acceptance, to contribute to something or the life of someone else and to have a reason for living. Most people want security. Engage in things that satisfy your deeper needs in a lasting way, and don't waste time with the temporary thrills of life.

QUESTIONS TO PONDER

1. Think about the process you experienced in finding out what you love. Are you still in the process of finding it?
2. How can this process stimulate your "sweet spot"?
3. How can you distinguish between activities with temporal and permanent pleasure?
4. Think about how you can engage in activities that are healthy, long-lasting and have a permanent effect.

HAPPINESS
choice is a

Finding your sweet spot will bring you happiness in life. Thankfully, access to the sweet spot is not some random process that chooses to work in some people and not in others. People's ability to access their sweet spot is not limited by what kind of genes they have or the cards they are dealt with in life. Finding your sweet spot and the happiness that you discover when you have found it are available to everyone. Like Kathleen and I share with our clients, happiness is a choice and I hope this book has efficiently demonstrated to you this important idea.

You can choose to entertain thoughts that your brain responds positively to, creating connections that will in turn stimulate the release of happy chemicals of a lasting kind.

We are all responsible for our choices and our thoughts. We have the ability to choose which thoughts we follow and which activities we participate in. You can see that you can also choose happiness by quieting your mind from the thoughts that are distractions or a waste of time. Remember that you are in control and can steer the conversations in your mind. This can be challenging for some people at first, however, it is possible if you put in work and it eventually becomes a habit.

We can choose to think negatively which stunts our growth. Most people who react negatively to things can easily be consumed by anger, hatred and aggression leading to domestic disputes and family separations.

90

On the other hand we can also choose to think positively, starting by choosing positive words over negative ones. You can choose to reshape your thinking and stop seeing the glass as half empty. You can choose to stop thinking something is wrong with you because you did not complete school; or most of your friends are married or in a relationship and you're not; or others around your age have a good career, make more money than you, own property, and so on. Learn to be content with yourself. Each tree brings forth its fruit in its own season. Wait for your season. Learn to count your blessings and be grateful for what you have, as the best is yet to come. Positivity will build a cloud of protection over your life. You have the choice to be like a bee that produces honey instead of stings, or like a lemon that makes sweet lemonade rather than one that stays sour.

You can choose what you spend your time on. Learn to occupy yourself rather than choosing to do nothing with your life. The more we can become active with stimulating challenges in our life, the more we help our brain work on our behalf and the more likely we are to find happiness. We can be happy from physical exercise, eating healthy, spending time with extended family and friends, going on vacation, volunteering, working in a field you love, studying, going to church, etc.. We are able to draw happiness from many different sources.

In anger management, people learn to study their anger and learn how to control themselves. They can become the most loving people. We should treat happiness the same. We need to find out what things trigger our happiness and pursue those things.

I like to encourage people to stop hindering their happiness by finding what they love and doing it. If happiness required changing the world around you, happiness would not be a choice. I learned when I was about seventeen I cannot change the world, but I can change myself. Changing the world around you is out of your control, but you can choose to change your choices. Luckily, that's all it takes to find true happiness.

When we first were married, it was very difficult to live with Kathleen as I was a perfectionist. It was terrible when I look back now, but I could not stand dishes in the sink, different types of dishes together or when they were put away such that they were not straightly lined up according to logical coordination. Shoes had to be positioned the right way in a line and the bed needed to be made up military style where a coin could bounce on it. My closets had to have all pants and shirts coordinated by colour. The living room had to have the television and sofa the right distance apart. Each window and door curtain had to look the same. I used to become very frustrated and ask myself what I had gotten myself into. I had to seek change in this area which I did when the children came along. God delivered me from this and kept my soul at peace. My happiness grew when I realized that it was okay not to be a perfectionist and I could change. Happiness was my choice.

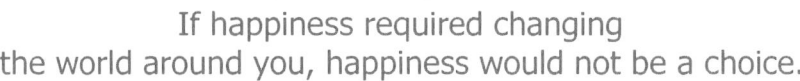

If happiness required changing
the world around you, happiness would not be a choice.

When I say happiness is a choice, I don't mean that you can make one decision and all of a sudden you're happy. Happiness is a choice because we can live happily by making a series of choices that together steer us towards happiness. How we live our lives and how we choose to react to the world will determine if we stay happy or allow our happiness to be crippled. We need to learn how to make room for what we love, dance in the rain, laugh in the midst of our troubles, cry with joy and sing in the storms of life. We choose to be happy and no one else can make that choice for us.

QUESTIONS TO PONDER

1. Who is responsible for our thoughts and choices?
2. If we cannot change the world around us who can we change?
3. Is happiness a choice? Can you choose someone else's happiness?
4. Take time to think about doing all the things you love and those who would love to share that with you.

mind at EASE

We all have learned that when the mind is at ease it's easier to keep thoughts positive and stay safe. In fact, when the mind is at ease a person feels safe and is able to be respectful and show appreciation to those around them. They are able to concentrate and stay focused on what they are doing, what they are saying or where they are going. They can be more caring and supportive.

The main purpose of all therapies is to teach the mind to stay focused and be at ease. At my clinic I have found that by asking some questions and having clients review and revisit the questions I can help them to put their minds at ease. Questions such as: Who are my supports? Why are there so many people interested in my life? How did I become like this? What has caused me to think this way? What can I do for myself to make an impression on my friends and family?

Sometimes simple homework like writing down their thoughts before going to bed or during the day, helps our clients to put their minds at ease. Some clients share how they feel and get themselves into altercations. Some have the people they hang around with, part ways with them. To put the mind at ease, it's always better to write the thoughts down instead of acting impulsively and saying something you regret.

We all have to learn how to make adjustments to our lives in order to be happy. We need to learn boundaries, learn to laugh, learn to share our hearts, compliment others, take compliments, share appreciation, give thanks, reflect on all the good you possess and in those who you care about. Stop over-thinking and trying to convince yourself, sit in the sun, go for a walk, enjoy the outdoors and look for opportunities.

The pointers in this book will guide you to put your mind at ease. We must choose positive thoughts, evaluate what we are learning and who we are learning from, trust ourselves that we are making the right decision, get second opinions, accept mistakes, and go easy on ourselves when things are not working out.

Clients who were interested in praying, reading a book, writing poetry, painting, fishing or allowing their thoughts to be focused on something else have expressed that their minds were relaxed and they felt refreshed.

Imagine a valuable, priceless vase sitting on a column where people can observe it. What would the protection around this vase look like? What would be appropriate to put the owner's mind at ease? Now think of your mind as being that vase and sitting in a place where people are observing. What safety net are you going to use to safeguard your mind?

Retraining your thought processes is a very important part of assisting someone to move ahead in their life and achieve healthy living. Now that we have a better understanding of the mind and how our brains work, let's put some of these therapies to work. Please keep in mind that there are many other forms of therapies that you may have heard of or participated in, that have some similar aspects to what is suggested in this book.

— ⚭ —

Retraining your thought processes is a
very important part of assisting someone to move ahead
in their life and achieve healthy living.

Not every person will get to their sweet spot. There are many people who are disappointed in life, some who wish they were not born, some who see no purpose, some who wish they could start all over again, some who have deep regrets and these can be very difficult to overcome. However, for what it's worth, there's not a good enough reason to stop trying.

I would like to list a few forms of supportive therapy that have helped others to overcome "being stuck in the mud." These therapies were able to help them break free and, I am sure, set off their sweet spots.

1. Behavioural therapies are used to help reduce unwanted behaviours through desensitization, rewards and reinforcements. Most parents use this form of therapy to some degree when raising their children. It helps in reducing anxiety, phobias and fears. It involves teaching and training a person to relax and understand why they feel the way they do and what can be done to implement safety. Usually along with the individual, friends and family need to be on board for success to be achieved.

2. Biomedical therapy is an alternative. You may have heard of the struggle some people have with being compliant in taking prescribed medications, especially those with mental illness. Medications and psychotherapy work hand in hand. Working with individuals to "see the light" (the need to take medications) proves this therapy to be potentially successful.

3. Client-centred therapy is based on the teaching of Carl Rogers. It's a teaching to support individuals with a wide range of issues, where the individual is the expert of his own life. The individual has the authority over their life and can explore their ideas, thoughts, feelings, choices and diagnoses to formulate a treatment plan. Individuals are encouraged to visualize the power they hold over their lives.

4. Cognitive Behavioural Therapy (CBT) teaches individuals to change negative thought patterns, behaviours and beliefs into

positive ones to manage their symptoms. Individuals learn how to feel positive emotions.

5. Family counselling involves working with couples and discussing what the causes of their issues are. Usually Kathleen and I teach couples how to open an emotional wound and explore what is causing the infections. After about five to fifteen weeks of therapy, we usually see healing as we provide the emotional antibiotics to bring healing.

6. Dialectical Behavioural Therapy (DBT) has been successful in supporting individuals with self-injury. This is useful with suicidal thoughts, drug dependences, eating disorders, etc. People learn how to accept themselves for who they are and yet the need for change is stressed. They learn how to become competent by giving up their negative thoughts and accepting the issues they are struggling with. The focus becomes learning how to reduce them. This therapy is usually used with individuals with a diagnosis of Borderline Personality Disorder, those who have difficulty with inappropriate behaviours and those who act impulsively.

7. Electro Convulsive Therapy (ECT) is a technique that uses low voltage to shock the brain. It reboots the brain and is used especially when all other therapies fail. It works mostly for individuals with acute mania, major depression or someone who is very likely to commit suicide.

8. Eye Movement Desensitization Reprocessing is a therapy used to create eye movements that mimic those of REM sleep. It creates the same form of brain waves during REM sleep while the person is awake. Individuals with ADHD/ADD have benefited from this form of therapy.

9. Group therapy usually runs with four to fifteen people with similar issues. It focuses on individuals learning from one another.

10. Holistic therapy is using medicine and alternative therapies such as yoga and acupuncture to treat and prevent diseases. It's about education and healing. It's about channelling the free force of energy that flows through the spirit, mind and body. It is safe and it promotes healthy spiritual, emotional, environmental, nutritional, physical and social living.

11. Mindfulness Therapy focuses on learning to "go within oneself." It involves learning to observe, increase awareness and be in control of your mind instead of letting your mind be in control of you. It is also learning to be in control of attention processes. Mindfulness is learning to combine a reasonable mind and an emotional mind to have a wise mind. A reasonable mind is about facts and logics, things that make sense. The emotional mind prevents one from thinking too rationally and allows impulsive behaviour at times. Individuals tend to regret the decisions made in the emotional mind. When a reasonable mind and an emotional mind are combined we have a wise mind informing our "gut" feelings. Ideally, it results in decisions that make sense according to facts. An example is grieving and yet functioning effectively. The emotional mind alone prevents one from moving ahead.

12. Pastoral counselling has been known to help individuals and families who are struggling in life. Spirituality is the foundational base of this form of counselling.

13. Psychotherapy is known to be a very successful form of counselling. It is long-term rather than supportive counselling, exploring the cause of a person's issues and working on solutions. Areas explored are social, physical and familial realms in addition to employment-related, medical, mental, educational, career-related and relational causes.

14. Psychoanalysis is one form of therapy that is intensive and long-term. It explores emotional and behavioural issues.

15. Rational Emotive Behavioural Therapy is a form of therapy that was first articulated by Dr. Albert Ellis in 1955. He thought of getting individuals to create their emotions by learning how to overcome their pasts and focus on their futures. It features the power to choose and work on embracing change to move ahead.

16. Reality Therapy is similar to REBT which was developed in the 1960's by William Glasser. The concept is teaching individuals that they have a choice to change their future. Individuals learn that their future is theirs and they can change their behaviour to make a difference. The five basic needs that are emphasized in this form of therapy are survival, love and belonging, power, freedom and fun. This therapy teaches personal responsibility and empowerment to make changes in order to satisfy a person's needs and wants.

17. My very own therapy which I call Thought Developmental Practice is a combination of most of the therapies included above. It's a twelve-week process of retraining the brain to develop new options as a diversion when stuck with addictions, anxiety and depression. I like to think that this therapy is educating the neurons in the brain to find alternative ways of coping with these. It's like storing "chips" in the brain with coping strategies.

    The process of helping others find happiness is not always easy. Despite all these forms of therapy, we see a need for more. There are still individuals who are struggling and are looking to find their sweet spot. There is always an assumption when supporting clients that they are doing the best they can and want to improve. There is also the assumption that clients can do better. They can try harder and become more motivated to change. We also consider that they may not try harder because of their issue. Clients cannot fail in therapy, but therapy can fail them. Some clients live with negative thoughts that can be unbearable. This leads to suicidal thoughts or other forms of coping like cutting, substance abuse, spending money or becoming inappropriately sexually active. Some clients punish themselves for other people's issues or issues that affect them. It is very easy to say "we will pray for you," but the issue will still exist until the solution comes.

Finding one's sweet spot can be challenging when someone is not in their right frame of mind and is in need of therapy. Individuals who live like failures and have failed to learn how to regulate and express or describe their emotions have difficulty learning how to tolerate any form of distress as their emotions have been seared.

People want to feel validated for their feelings and issues they carry and may not know how to get validation. Many struggle with communication and expressing their feelings. Some have tried every form of counselling, medical treatment and suggestions made by friends, families and even professionals yet still feel like they are in the same position as before. They may have completed a 360-degree turn and gone back to where they started.

There are a number of things I experienced in the process of finding my sweet spot that I would like to share. There are some hard lessons you'll have to learn even if you are not afflicted to the point of mental illness.

1. In my journey to discover my sweet spot, I can recall that not everyone liked me. I had to fight with that reality and still do to some extent. People won't like you for many reasons: your habits, your skin colour, your culture, your character, your personality, your faith, how you dress, the food you eat, you name it. It is helpful to accept this. You never have to feel you must change in order for others to like you. You need to be the person God created you to be. If the reason relates to bad habits or negative actions then that's a different story.

2. You'll need help as you try to implement change in your life. Learn to "kill your pride" and ask for help. This goes especially

for men. I remember before GPS came out, Kathleen and I would go travelling and when we got lost I found it difficult to ask for directions. We would have a problem like a broken faucet and I knew I could fix it, however I had time constraints. It would have been easy to call someone to fix it, but my pride stood in the way. This can happen in your studies, relationships and place of employment. There is no need to feel that asking for help will change you as a person.

3. Be honest with yourself and accept that you don't always have to be right or have the answers to everything. Sometimes we feel if we don't do things by the book, we are failures and we become stressed over the littlest things. We can only do so much and must come to accept our flaws. We are not perfect and should not feel pressured to be. Acknowledge your strengths and weaknesses. Examine your gifts and talents and focus on them.

4. Be open to feeling the full range of emotions. Learn to smile, cry, laugh, express sympathy, show affection and sorrow as things come your way. It will give you freedom.

5. I remember I used to compare myself with others. While it was a form of motivation, there were many times I felt like a failure, especially with guys who were around my age. Sometimes I would avoid speaking to guys around my age to avoid conversations that would expose my heart. I soon realized that there were many men who were motivated by me and I did not have to compare myself with others, but work on myself. So many of us compare ourselves with others whether it's about the clothes others wear, the type of homes they have, their spouses, their children, their jobs, their education. The temptation to compare will come, but we should never give in unless it's a matter of motivation. We should all be living to better ourselves and we can use others as examples, however, we should be content with what we have.

6. Stand up for what you believe in. Sometimes we think humility means being a doormat for someone else to walk on. We need to stand up for ourselves and what we believe in. I remember I stood up for myself in one class while I was in university. No one else wanted to take a stand for their beliefs, but talked about how much they disagreed with the professor. The professor failed me, although I did well in this class. I asked for a review and rewrote the test, and got a passing mark of 92%. Once the dean became aware of the situation and requested a rewrite, my answer spoke for itself. I felt like I owned a million bucks. I stood up for myself.

7. Another important concept is finding quality people who believe in you and treat you with respect and dignity. It's difficult to find people who would invest their time in your life without any returns. But it is important to find such people, those who you can have honest, open conversations without becoming anxious. People who will give seasoned advice and have proven themselves in their own lives can usually be trusted with advice about wise choices.

It is possible to put your mind at ease. There are many forms of therapy available. Set-backs and particularly tough challenges may come, but knowing that these are a part of any successful process and being ready for the types of challenges you might face will help you put your mind at ease and keep your sweet spot sweet in the long-term.

QUESTIONS TO PONDER

1. What happens to a person when their mind is put at ease?
2. Name a few therapies listed in this chapter that you found very interesting.
3. What are some hard lessons you may have to learn?

4. It is always important to find those that believe in you. Name some people who have invested in your life and that have been examples to you.

conclusion:
be good to
YOUR **brain**

Get your brain working on your behalf by doing the things that stimulate happiness. The main purpose of this book was to identify what makes someone happy from a scientific perspective by employing the brain and working with one's thoughts to find permanent happiness which I believe lies in the brain. The brain is a great and complex organ and works by certain principles. We can't just live our lives anyhow and expect to find happiness because happiness involves triggering the release of chemicals in this majestic and mysterious organ.

There are a number of things we can do to set the process of triggering our sweet spot in motion. Don't abuse your brain by keeping it "on" and going a mile a minute all of the time. Organize your life because your organized brain responds positively to organization and structure. Find what you love to do and make a career of it.

When people switch jobs, educational paths, faiths, countries, social groups, relationship partners and friends, when they engage in clubbing, illicit drug use and thrills, happiness is what they are looking for. Happiness is what the world is looking for.

Understanding ourselves is the number one rule in finding happiness. We need to be honest with who we are, our limitations, experiences, skills and knowledge. We need to conclude that not everyone will like us, not everyone will agree with our perspective in life, not everyone will agree with our thoughts, our choices or our decisions. We need to be content with what we have and what we need to move ahead, not depending on others, but when the help comes we should take it. We piggy back on those who have already paved the way and work towards making new pathways in life.

The study of the brain, our thoughts and how we function was the key I found to help me be true to myself. I consider myself to be happy, especially when I trigger the sweet spot. My brain releases happy chemicals which keep my smile on regardless of the negative thoughts, bad days and obstacles that stand in my path.

My personal recommendation to everyone is to "find their sweet spot." This is what people are looking for and some will do anything to find it. Now knowing how the brain works, what combination of things can you do that will bring you happiness? We are all different yet find pleasure and happiness in some of the same areas of life. This book has explored some areas that you can further explore. Finding your sweet spot will give you a permanent high better than the best drug out on the streets. It is the only "high" that brings the contentment. It's legal, safe and others will support you.

My brain releases happy chemicals which keep my smile on regardless of the negative thoughts, bad days and obstacles that stand in my path.

Once you discover the sweet spot, people will want what you have and will draw close to you like bears to honey. You will feel like nothing can stand in your path as you see life through a different set of lenses than most people. Your brain will operate on higher levels. You will learn to train this marvelous organ to remember names, numbers, and places. You will be a source of inspiration and a blessing to others.

I hope this book was a blessing to you as writing it was a blessing to me. Learning about ourselves and why we do what we do can help us make wise decisions. Once you know how to grab a hold of that sweet spot, you are always in control of your life unless you give it away to someone else. No one can bring happiness to you, but yourself. No one can discover your sweet spot but yourself. Making good choices will draw you closer to your sweet spot—choices that respect the bounds of your brain and align with what makes it tick.

about the author

Harrison S. Mungal, PhD, is considered one of the leading cognitive therapist workshop presenters in the world. He has been a guest speaker in over thirty-four nations on several radio station and television programs, for the Attorney General of Canada, the police, hospitals, and community agencies. He is appreciated for the depth of his knowledge, great humour and passion in the field of mental health. In addition, he is also an expert for supporting the development of healthy relationships and happy parenting. He utilizes a creative science-based approach to deliver compelling presentations which have granted him a great reputation. He has received several awards and honours from the local police, mayor, community leaders, managers and directors as well as families.

Dr. Mungal provides training and consultations to an array of community partners including psychiatrists, medical doctors, social workers, nurses, police officers and senior management teams. He has his own private practice with several interns under his supervision. He has over twenty years of professional experience working with diverse populations. Some of these diverse populations include youth and adult offenders, communities impacted by acquired brain injuries, refugees, war victims and crisis-based support groups.

Dr. Mungal holds a bachelor's degree in Theology, two master's degrees (MA, MSW), and a PhD. He is a founding member of the Canadian Association of Cognitive and Behavioural Therapies; and also a member of the Ontario Psychological Association; the Ontario College of Social Workers and Social Service Workers; the Canadian Association of Neuroscience; and the American Society of Neuroscience.

books written by Dr. Mungal

Dr. Harrison S. Mungal

DIVERGENT
ISBN: 978-1-9278-6528-6
Learning the difference between thinking in divergent and convergent ways helps us to understand ourselves better and to process what enters our minds for our success. Divergent thinking will help you to move into your destiny, to arrive at quick solutions to personal struggles and to develop untapped creativity. This book will teach you that your brain is one of the best tools you have to steer your future in the right direction.

TURTLE ON A FENCE POST
ISBN: 978-1-9278-6515-6
Children need to see that it is sometimes okay to disagree with their parents, and that their parents are not perfect and they can expect them to fail. Most parents want the best for their children, however, a parent's approach may not be what a child needs. What should be the role of a parent? What should be the role of a child? How can parents equip their children for a bright future? These topics and more explored in *Turtle on a Fence Post*.

KISSING BREAKUPS GOODBYE
ISBN: 978-1-4866-0754-9
This book will address some of the causes behind poor choices and discuss how devastating the consequences can be in our relationships. It will help couples consider the effects before they make irrational decisions. Every one of us has power over our hearts. We can come to a place where we are moved not by how we feel, but by the decisions we make. Regardless of who we are, we need to take into consideration the consequences.

COLD SHOWERS ARE CHEAPER THAN A DIVORCE
ISBN: 978-1-4866-0759-4
Cold Showers are Cheaper than a Divorce will help individuals and couples to see the bigger picture in any relationship by reflecting on some major areas of contention that can affect their future together. The major cause of divorce revolves around sex, so it leads us to understand why sex is an issue that needs to be addressed, even though most people feel uncomfortable talking about it. This book will bring about a better understanding regarding the main struggles that couples face in their relationships.

WHEN LOVE COMES BACK
ISBN: 978-1-4866-0764-8
In this book you will discover the need to spend time with your children, the consequences of not investing time with them, and the legacy of what can happen from your children falling in love with you. You will discover what the requirements are for love to become evident in your relationship with your children, the necessities of sowing and reaping that are implemented in the relationship, and the entitlement of being a proud parent.

GET YOUR FAMILY INTO THE ARK
SBN: 978-1-4866-0769-3
We are living in a fast-paced society. Parents are working, some with multiple jobs. Children are sometimes also working and can be enrolled in school at the same time. The family is being pulled apart by the demands of our society. What are some of the consequences families face as a result of these demands? What are the necessary tools that are needed to keep the family together? This book will provide parents with concepts that will help them to keep their family together in our busy and demanding society.

MUSIC THERAPY AND MENTAL ILLNESS: WITH A FOCUS ON SCHIZOPHRENIA AND THE ROLE OF PASTORS
ISBN: 978-1-46910-2962
With the increasingly important role of psychosocial interventions in the treatment of schizophrenia and other mental illness, many interventions have been adequately researched and standardized to meet the criteria for evidence-based practice. Music therapy is one such modality, which is viewed as another therapeutic form of intervention. However, there was previously no resource to guide music therapists in the implementation of appropriate evidence-based techniques. This book develops such a resource, which matches psychosocial goals with appropriate music therapy interventions across the domains of functioning.

To book Dr. Harrison and Kathleen Mungal for speaking engagements or counselling sessions, please call 905-533-1334 or send an email to hsmungal@hotmail.com.